About the Author

NFT TRENDING .COM

NftTrending.com is a British Crypto Art News and Busness Website

based in London, England.

NFT Trending is a collective, we used to consult global brands on crypto headquartered in central London and Silicon Valley California. Although now we would say we've found a more fulfilling role in life: coaching clients from around the world, changing lives for the better and when we're not travelling or surviving global pandemics, we try to find time to write about how success can happen.

We are in the changing lives business.

Join Our

NFT Crypto Art & DEFI Entrepenuer

Power Group

To help reinforce the learning's from our books, I strongly suggest you join our well-informed powerhouse community on Facebook.

Here, you will connect and share with other like-minded people to support your journey and help you grow.

>>>Click here to join Our Personal Growth Support Group

<<<

News Site Here:

https://www.facebook.com/NFT-Trending-104426528387351

Community Group:

https://www.facebook.com/groups/nfttrending/

NFT

Investing For Beginners

(Non Fungible Tokens)

to Advanced.

By NFT Trending

Table of Contents

CHAPTER 1: NFT ESSENTIALS..1

CHAPTER 2: HOW NFT WORKS..17

CHAPTER 3: NEW NFT INVESTMENTS.......................................32

CHAPTER 4: FUTURE COLLECTIBLES......................................46

CHAPTER 5: ASSET CATEGORIES...65

CHAPTER 6: ETHEREUM AND THE FUTURE OF NFTS........................80

CHAPTER 7: CO-INVESTING IN ART AND LUXURY COLLECTIBLES...91

CHAPTER 8: SUCCESS & FAILURES.. 102

CHAPTER 9: HOW TO BE A CRYPTO ARTIST 119

CHAPTER 10: LEGITIMATE MARKETPLACES........................ 138

CHAPTER 11: NEW NFT MARKETS...147

CHAPTER 12: ENVIRONMENTAL POSITIVE CRYPTO.......................... 162

CONCLUSION 179

Chapter 1:
NFT ESSENTIALS

Concept of NFTs

Recently, the word NFT has been all over the news, frequently in connection with large amounts of money. However, you might be wondering what all the buzz is about. We're here to guide you if you're not clear of what NFT – or non-fungible token – is all about. This guide will teach you all you need to understand regarding NFTs, including what they are, how they are mined and traded, why they've sparked debate, and how you can be a part of the buzz.

Generally, an NFT is a collectible digital asset with value both as crypto and as a piece of art or valued item. NFTs are being seen as a value-holding investment in the same way that art is. But how do you do it?

Let's start with a definition of the term. NFT stands for non-fungible token, which is a form of crypto similar to Bitcoin and Ethereum. However, unlike a regular coin on the blockchain network, an NFT is one-of-a-kind and cannot be traded for other NFTs (hence, non-fungible).

So, what distinguishes an NFT from a standard cryptocurrency? The file contains additional information, elevating it above mere currency and allowing it to be used for anything. NFTs come in various shapes and sizes, but they may be a piece of digital art or an ancient antique – something special that can be stored digitally and considered valuable. In essence, they are similar to any other tangible collector's object, except that instead of artwork on canvas to display on your wall, you receive a JPG file in your device storage.

Current NFTs Users

NFTs are certainly having a moment, with artists, gamers, and brands from all walks of life contributing to the trend. In reality, it appears that a new player enters the NFT market every day. Stepping into the NFT world provides artists with a new space and medium to create and share their art, as well as a new way for their fans to embrace their work. Artists can give the public a variety of ways to purchase art and make money, with works ranging from tiny, quick-to-create GIFs to more creative works.

Until now, all digital assets purchased inside a game belonged to the game company, with players only purchasing them to use them when playing the game. However, NFTs imply that asset ownership has transferred to the buyer, allowing them to be purchased and sold around the gaming network with added value depending on who has owned them previously. In reality, games based solely on NFTs are now being created, demonstrating how they are reshaping the industry.

Popular artists are entitled to be compensated handsomely for their work, which is exactly what happened when an unknown group of 'art enthusiasts' burned an initial Banksy to convert it into an NFT. Other sales, on the other hand, are more shocking. It was, for instance, Beeple's first entry into the NFT industry. Despite his popularity as a digital artist, the fact that this sale fetched one of the most lucrative prices ever paid for a living artist was unexpected.

And NFTs are a lucrative revenue source for businesses, as evidenced by the recent flurry of brand adoption. Taco Bell sold taco-themed GIFs and images on one market, and the entire stock of 25 sold out in less than 30 minutes. Each NFT came with a $500 gift card that the original owner could use, contributing to their initial success. These TacoCards, on the other hand, are now being sold on the secondary market, with the most valuable card fetching $3,500. That does not include the gift card, just to be specific.

NBA Top Shot is a route for the NBA to sell digital collectibles in trading cards that feature awesome game moments. The NBA is looking for ways to grow this income stream as far as it can go, with plans to add virtual jewelry, shoes, and apparel that can be used through social media. Even tweets are valuable, as Twitter co-founder Jack Dorsey just sold the first-ever tweet for $2,915,835.47.

You could also purchase digital real estate and 3D assets, including furniture from artists who are selling the ownership and originals of their songs, as well as short videos to clips of their songs. In reality, a 'digital house' was recently sold for an incredible $500,000. The 'first digital house in the world,' according to digital art market SuperRare, is Toronto artist Krista Kim's 'Mars House.' The owner will be able to navigate the house on Mars through virtual reality, including sunbathing outside the building, thanks to the help of an architect and video game tech.

Buzzwords

Decentralized Exchange (DEX)

Exchange does not require users to deposit funds until they can begin trading and not keep their funds. Users instead exchange directly from their wallets.

Decentralized Autonomous Organization (DAO)

Decentralized Autonomous Organization is abbreviated as DAO. A Decentralized Autonomous Organization (DAO) is a set of hard-coded guidelines that describe the actions that a decentralized organization will take. Nevertheless, DAO may also apply to an entity known as "The DAO," founded in 2016 on the Ethereum blockchain.

Blockchain

A blockchain, in a nutshell, is a digital, ever-growing list of data records. A list like this comprises numerous data blocks ordered in chronological order and connected and protected by cryptographic proofs.

Decentralized Finance (DeFi)

DeFi stands for "decentralized finance," which refers to the network of financial applications designed on top of blockchain platforms. Decentralized finance (DeFi) is a trend that encourages the application of open-source software and decentralized networks to build a variety of financial services and goods. The aim is to develop and run financial DApps on a transparent and trustless foundation, such as permissionless blockchains and other peer-to-peer (P2P) protocols.

Smart Contracts

A smart contract is a form of computer software that acts as an automatic self-enforcing contract, meaning that it takes action when specific requirements are met. Smart contracts may be used as digital agreements between two entities to facilitate the transfer of cryptocurrencies (or any other digital product).

The smart contract verifies that the terms of the deal have been met, and the properties are allocated accordingly.

Initial Coin Offering (ICO)

The Initial Coin Offering (ICO) is a novel method of raising funds using digital currencies (cryptocurrencies). An approach like this is more common in cryptocurrency ventures that haven't wholly built their blockchain-based product, service, or system. The funds raised at ICO events are usually obtained in Bitcoin (BTC) or Ether (ETH), although fiat currency could also be accepted in some instances.

Bitcoin

A cryptographic-secured digital currency is widely used to exchange in a peer-to-peer (P2P) digital economic system. These frameworks are resistant to fraud and counterfeiting thanks to the use of cryptographic methods.

Nodes

The meaning of a node varies depending on the situation. In computer or telecommunication networks, nodes may serve as either a redistribution point or a communication endpoint. A node is typically made up of a physical network computer, though virtual nodes are also used.

Cryptography

In a nutshell, cryptography is the art of concealing data. Modern cryptography, in particular, employs mathematical techniques and computation to encrypt and decrypt data and ensure the security and validity of data.

Exchange

This is a controlled platform for trading financial items such as cryptocurrency, goods, and securities . A actual site or a digital platform can be used to facilitate an exchange. Many traditional exchanges that used to only enable in-person trading now have digitized networks which allow digital trading (also known as paperless trading).

Crypto wallet

In a nutshell, a crypto wallet is a platform for interacting with a blockchain network. Numerous crypto wallet forms can be classified into three categories: software, hardware, and paper wallets. They are also known as hot or cold wallets, depending on their working principle.

Altcoin

A non-Bitcoin cryptocurrency. There are thousands of altcoins, each with its own set of values and applications.

AML

Anti-money laundering (AML) is a series of rules, legislation, and protocols to stop criminals from passing off illegally acquired funds as legal earnings.

Blocks

Transactional data is stored in these files. Blocks are identical to the pages of a ledger.

Bubble

Whenever the price of a product becomes inflated, it outperforms its true value. When a bubble bursts, rates plummeted.

Decentralized

Bitcoin is a decentralized network since several different miners protect the network compared to a centralized network, like banking. A body, such as the central bank, makes the decisions.

Digital Asset

A digital asset is self-contained, distinctly recognizable, and has a meaning or capacity to use in binary data.

Digital Signature

A digital code is applied to an electronically transmitted document to validate its contents and the sender's identity (generated and validated using public-key encryption).

Futures Contract

A futures contract is a contractual legal arrangement between unrelated parties to buy or sell something at a fixed price at a future date. The asset traded is typically a product or financial instrument.

Futures Exchange

A futures exchange, also known as a futures market, is a centralized financial exchange whereby individuals may trade structured futures contracts that the exchange has specified.

Github

GitHub is a web-based version-control and collaboration platform for computer programmers. It was established in 2008 and is based on Git, an open-source code management framework developed by Linus Torvalds to make software develops faster.

Gas

On the Ethereum blockchain network, the fee or pricing value is needed to perform a transaction or implement a contract effectively.

KYC

Know-your-customer (KYC) is a compliance mechanism used to check the validity of a company's customers before or around the time they begin doing business with them. Financial companies are required by law to use KYC procedures when onboarding new customers.

Mining

Miners devote computer hardware to process transactions on a blockchain (Bitcoin or other cryptocurrencies) in exchange for mining bonuses and benefits.

Mining Farm

A mining farm is a data center that is technically designed to mine Bitcoins or other cryptocurrencies. Mining farms arise due to the mining process becoming more complicated, necessitating more technological, energy, and financial resources.

Off-Chain

Off-chain transactions are those that take place on a cryptocurrency network and transfer value away from the blockchain.

On-Chain

On-chain transactions are cryptocurrency transactions that take place on the blockchain - that is, on the blockchain's records - and whose legitimacy is determined by the nature of the blockchain.

P2P

Peer-to-peer (P2P) networks are made up of computer systems linked to each other via the internet and allow files to be exchanged freely between them without a central server.

Proof of Work (POW

Proof of work is a protocol aimed at preventing cyber-attacks such as a distributed denial-of-service attack (DDoS) that aims to drain a computer system's resources by sending several bogus requests.

Proof of Stake (POS)

Proof of stake would fully virtualize the consensus process. While the entire procedure is similar to the proof of work (POW), the mechanism for achieving the end goal is distinct. POW miners use their computing tools to solve cryptographically complex puzzles

Token

In general, a token is a cryptocurrency that is not supported by its blockchain but instead relies on another currency's blockchain features, such as ERC20 tokens, which are supported by Ethereum smart contracts.

Importance of NFTs

Non-fungible tokens are a step forward from the relatively straightforward definition of cryptocurrencies. Modern finance systems provide complex exchange and investment systems for various asset categories, including real estate, artwork, and music. NFTs are progressing in the revival of this system because they allow digital representations of tangible assets.

Specifically, neither the concept of digital representations of tangible assets nor the application of unique identification is new. When merged with the advantages of a rigid blockchain of smart contracts, these ideas become a powerful force for reform.

Business quality is perhaps the most apparent advantage of NFTs. Converting a tangible asset to a virtual asset simplifies procedures and eliminates mediators. NFTs reflect virtual or physical artwork on a blockchain, removing the need for representatives and allowing artists to interact directly with their fan base. They can also help businesses develop their processes. An NFT for a beer bottle, for instance, would make it easier for various players in the supply chain to communicate with it and monitor its authenticity, development, and selling during the process. Ernst & Young, a consulting company, has already created a similar solution for its customers.

Non-fungible tokens are equally great for managing identities. Take a look at the case of physical passports, which must be shown at any point of entry and exit. It is possible to simplify the entry and exit systems for countries by transforming each passport into NFTs, each with its special identifying features. NFTs may also be used for identity management in the digital world, expanding on this use case.

By fractionalizing tangible assets like property investment, NFTs can equally decentralize investment. A digital property investment asset is much simpler to share among multiple holders than a tangible one. This tokenization practice does not have to be limited to real estate; it can be applied to other properties as well, including artwork. As a result, a painting does not always require a single owner. Its digital counterpart can have several owners, each responsible for a small portion of the work. Such agreements could boost the company's value and revenue.

The emergence of new opportunities and forms of investment is the most promising possibility for NFTs. Imagine a tract of land that has been divided into several parts, each with its own set of features and property types. One division might be located near a beach, while another is is a shopping center, and another is a residential neighborhood. Each piece of land is special, valued separately, and depicted by an NFT based on its features. By integrating necessary metadata into each specific NFT, real estate trading can be streamlined, which is a complicated and cumbersome process.

Myth Surrounding NFTs

I'd like to clarify any misconceptions regarding NFTs. They aren't complex, pointless, or a waste of money.

- **NFTs are Complex**

NFTs are a form of crypto token representing true ownership of a digital asset, like a work of digital art. NFTs are often used to denote provenance. That is, every NFT includes a history of a digital asset's ownership. Collectors should be assured that their investment is safe since only one copy can be traced back to its owner.

The animated flying-cat image has been displayed and posted hundreds of millions of times since Chris Torres produced it a decade ago. When he placed a special version of the image up for auction as an NFT on Foundation, it sparked a bidding war, with a collector paying about $580,000 for it. The collector can rest easy knowing that he owns the only special copy of this NFT.

Collectors are drawn to NFT art because of its scarcity due to the notion that there is only one of any object. Since each NFT is completely special, its meaning is derived solely from the features that make it. That might seem complicated, but it isn't. From a logical standpoint, it's no different than a blank canvas. If I paint on it, it will only be worth anything to my mother because it will be absolutely special due to my added characteristics. It's a commercially viable commodity if Andy Warhol does it.

- **NFTs is a Wrong Investment**

We've learned many times in the art world that art is a poor investment because it is difficult to turn to cash and is mostly speculative. In the art world, drastic rises in the price of a few amazing pieces can obscure the fact that the worth of several other works is declining. The same can be said for NFTs. This is true for all speculative assets.

Investing in original works and having a good provenance is the perfect way to make good NFT investments. Not every asset can appreciate dramatically, and that isn't the target. Risk management is the goal: Assets of high value and provenance are less likely to depreciate. A few items in a good collection can appreciate quickly, while the rest will at least sustain their value.

- **NFTs are Extremely Pointless**

It took a bit of time for NFTs to gain widespread recognition. The traditional art world's misconception of NFTs as merely a digital art phenomenon may have slowed their ascent.

In reality, there isn't anything here that is novel. Modern art has a long association with digital art. Legendary artists have been experimenting with this platform since the rise of the digital era. Visual art exhibits are well-known at internationally renowned institutions such as the Centre Pompidou in Paris.

Nevertheless, until now, this type of art has been challenging to monetize with NFTs. The future of NFTs and art is promising as the exposure and revenue produced have prompted traditional artists (who could still favor canvas and paintbrush) to incorporate new digital elements into their work.

- **Forgery and Misattribution**

Validating the uniqueness and legitimacy of digital arts is a common problem, particularly as the cost of counterfeit and pirated products keeps rising. This is where the blockchain enters the equation. The blockchain establishes a simple chain of titles when the crypto is an NFT. As a result, collectors can be assured that the digital file they have is the one-and-only "authentic."

Chapter 2:
HOW NFT WORKS

Characteristics of NFTs:

- **Non-interoperable**

CryptoPunks cannot be utilized as characters in the CryptoKitties game, and vice versa. This includes collectibles such as trading cards; a Blockchain Hero card can not be used in the Gods Unchained trading card game.

- **Indivisible**

Unlike bitcoin satoshis, NFTs are unitary and cannot be divided into different portions. They solely appear in a unit.

- **Indestructible**

Each token cannot be lost, deleted, or reproduced since all NFT data is preserved on the blockchain through blockchain technology. The possession of these tokens is also unchangeable, implying that gamers and holders own their NFTs rather than the companies that make them. This contrasts with purchasing music from the iTunes store, where consumers do not necessarily own the music they are buying; instead, they are purchasing permission to listen to it.

- **Verifiable**

Another advantage of storing past ownership data on the blockchain is that objects like digital art can be traced back to the original maker, eliminating the need for third-party authentication.

- **Unique**

The information tab on NFTs is extensive and demonstrates their uniqueness. This information is completely safe and accurate.

- **Limited**

The scarcity of NFTs adds to their value. NFT creators can generate an infinite number of NFTs, and they often alter the tokens to maximize interest.

- **Standardization**

Traditional digital assets, such as tickets and domain names, lack a single digital representation. A game's in-game collectibles are likely represented differently than an event ticketing process. Moreover, various games have specific standards. Developers can create universal, reusable, inheritable standards for all NFTs by representing them on blockchain networks.

These are similar to other digital building blocks such as the JPEG or PNG picture file format, HTTP for inter-computer requests, and HTML / CSS for web content display. On top of that, blockchain technologies add a layer that provides developers with a whole new collection of stateful primitives to construct applications on.

- **Tradeability**

Free exchange on open markets like OpenSea or Rarible is the most persuasive function allowed by interoperability. Participants can now transfer products out of their existing spaces and into an open market, where they can leverage advanced trading features such as eBay-style sales, bidding, bundling, and the ability to sell in any currency, including stablecoins and application-specific currencies.

Tradeability of assets reflects a shift from a closed economy to an open, free-market system for game developers. From resource availability to pricing to capital management, game developers no longer have to handle any aspect of their economy. It essentially refers to the shift from a planned economy to a free-market economy.

- **Transparency**

Blockchain technology cryptographic magic ensures the immutability and scarcity of NFTs. Since blockchain networks are open-source platforms, anyone can check that these digital promises are maintained. This openness is important for ensuring that a non-fungible token is truly unique and not reproduced.

- **Composability & Programmability**

Of course, NFTs are completely programmable, much like conventional digital assets. CryptoKitties included a breeding mechanism in the contract that reflects the digital cats. Many modern NFTs have more advanced dynamics, such as forging, crafting, redeeming, random creation, and so on. The design world is brimming with possibilities. To put it another way, the design world is very comprehensible since different projects will gain from each other, and there can be a lot of cross-fertilization. A crypto art NFT, for instance, is currently on display in a virtual gallery in Decentraland or the Sandbox (two digital spaces)

NFTs are extremely composable due to their programmable structure, and a wide range of interactions and variations can and will occur.

NFTs Scarcity

The maker of an NFT is in charge of determining the asset's scarcity. Consider purchasing a ticket to a football match. The maker of an NFT may choose how many replicas there are, just like an event manager can decide the number of tickets to sell.

5000 General Admission tickets, for example, are often exact replicas. A ticket with an allocated seat, for example, can be issued in multiples that are very identical yet differs slightly. In another scenario, the creator may desire to make a one-of-a-kind NFT as a unique collectible.

Each NFT will also have a specific identifier (like a bar code on a standard "ticket") and only one holder in these scenarios. The NFTs' planned scarcity is important, and it is up to the maker to decide. A creator may aim to make each NFT completely unique in order to create scarcity, or they could have solid reasons to produce thousands of replicas. Bear in mind that all of this information is freely accessible to the public.The Blockchain Technology

Concept of Blockchain

A blockchain is a set of interrelated blocks that store data. The strategy is developed to digital index records so that they cannot be backdated or tempered. Blockchain aims to eliminate the need for a central server to resolve the problem of duplicate records.

The blockchain is often used to securely transfer things such as money, assets, contracts, and other information without the need for an intermediary entity such as a bank or government. It is extremely difficult to alter data after it has been stored in a blockchain. The blockchain is a computer program (like

SMTP is for email). Blockchains, on the other hand, do not function without the Internet. It's also known as meta-technology because it affects other technologies. It comprises many components, including a database, a software program, and some related devices.

The word is often used to refer to the cryptocurrency blockchains, while other times, it relates to other virtual currencies or digital tokens. However, the majority of them will be discussing distributed ledgers.

The Architecture of the Blockchain

Now, let's look at the Blockchain architecture and its major elements in this Blockchain Technology

What is a block?

A blockchain is a series of interconnected blocks that store data. The type of blockchain determines the data that is stored within a block. A Bitcoin Block, for instance, provides information about the sender, receiver, and the number of bitcoins to be exchanged.

The Genesis block is the first link in the chain. Each new block in the chain is connected to the one before it.

Hash SHA256

A hash is also a part of something like a block. It can be thought of as a unique fingerprint for each block. It uniquely recognizes a block and all of its contents, similar to a fingerprint. As a result, once a block is generated, any change inside the block will change the hash.

What is SHA256?

As a result, the hash is extremely helpful in detecting changes in intersections. If a block's fingerprint varies, it is no longer the very same block.

Each Block consists of a Hash of the previous block's data.

Consider the following scenario, in which we have a three-block chain. There is no predecessor to the first block. As a result, it is missing the previous block. A hash of block 1 is found in block 2. Block 3 includes the Hash from block 2. As a result, all blocks contain hashes from previous blocks. This is the method that ensures the security of a blockchain.

Let's take a look at how it works. Suppose an attacker can alter the data in Block 2. As a result, the Hash of the Block changes as well. However, Block 3 still includes the Block 2 Hash. As a result, Block 3 and all subsequent blocks are useless since the previous block's hash is incorrect. As a result, modifying one block will easily render all subsequent blocks invalid.

Proofs of Work

Hashes are a great way to avoid tampering. However, today's computers are fast and can measure many hashes per second. An attacker may tamper with a block and then adjust all the hashes of other blocks to render the blockchain legitimate again in a couple of minutes.

Proof-of-Work is a term used by blockchains to prevent this problem. It's a process that delays the development of new blocks. A proof-of-work is an algorithmic problem that requires a certain amount of effort to resolve. However, relative to the effort needed to resolve the algorithmic problem, the time needed to check the results of the algorithmic problem is insignificant.

In the case of Bitcoin, calculating the necessary proof-of-work to add a new block to the chain takes nearly 10 minutes. In our example, if an attacker wanted to manipulate data in Block 2, he'd have to first execute proof of work (which would take 10 minutes) before making changes in Block 3 and subsequent blocks.

This system makes tampering with the blocks difficult because even though you tamper with one block, you'll have to adjust the proof-of-work for all subsequent blocks. As a result of hashing and the proof-of-work process, a blockchain is stable.

How Blockchain Transaction Works?

Step 1:

A transaction is required to get started. Crypto, contracts, documents, or other details may be involved in the transaction.

Step 2:

With the aid of nodes, the required transaction is broadcasted to a peer-to-peer network.

Step 3:

Using a well-known algorithm, the network of nodes validates the transaction and the user's status.

Step 4:

After the transaction is completed, a new block is added to the blockchain. The block is added in a way that is both eternal and unchangeable.

Blockchain Versions

Now, let's learn about Blockchain versions in Blockchain development

Blockchain 1.0: Currency

DLT (distributed ledger technology) contributed to the technology's first and most evident use: cryptocurrencies. This makes it possible to conduct financial transactions using blockchain technology. It's a money and a payment system. The most well-known instance of this category is Bitcoin.

Blockchain 2.0: Smart Contract

Smart Contracts are simple computer software that "run" in the blockchain, which is the latest main concept. They are open-access computer software that runs in the background and searches for conditions such as facilitation, verification, and compliance. It's a contract that's used to replace conventional contracts.

Blockchain 3.0: DApps (Decentralized application)

The backend code of the blockchain is distributed through a decentralized P2P network. A DApp, like a conventional app, can have frontend Blockchain example code and user interfaces developed in any language which can call its backend.

Public Blockchains

Ledgers in this form of blockchain are open to everybody on the web. Everyone can check a block of transactions and connect it to the blockchain. Individuals are encouraged to enter public networks, which are often free to use. Anyone can use a public blockchain network.

Private Blockchain

Only a community of organizations can validate and add transactions in this Blockchain version. The ledger may be made public or limited to exclusive classes. A variety of organizations uses the blockchain consortium. Only pre-authorized nodes have control over it.

Ethereum Cryptocurrency

The Ethereum blockchain (also known as 'Blockchain 2.0') is based on the same technology as Bitcoin, although it is more sophisticated. It has much more capabilities than the Bitcoin blockchain.

How Ethereum Works

Ethereum's token is called Ether. The two are often confused, but it's easier to note that Ethereum is the network and Ether is the coin.

You'll require Ether if you have to get something done on the network. Since Ether powers the Ethereum network, it's sometimes referred to as "gas." On the Ethereum platform, each transaction requires a specific amount of 'gas' to execute. The more work you have, the more gas you'll need.

Ether

Returning to the concept of Ethereum and its coin: Ether is a digital currency that powers the Ethereum platform's decentralized smart contracts. John may use an Ethereum smart contract to pay Michael 10ETH to paint his room. The payment will be as follows: IF Michael paints John's room, Michael will receive 10 ETH. As you can see, Ether works similarly to Bitcoin. With smart contract support, John will not pay Michael until Michael has painted John's room. Michael will not be paid unless he paints John's room, so he cannot cheat! This same mechanism can direct all sorts of transactions, from emails to how a business pays its employees.

Ethereum Mining

A method known as 'mining' is used to create new coins (Cryptocurrency) in Bitcoin, Ethereum, etc. On a blockchain network, nodes must validate transactions in exchange for a new currency. An Ethereum node (also known as a miner) is compensated with a new Ether.

Since it's close to gold or diamond mining, it's referred to as mining. The miners, on the other hand, are checking transactions rather than digging in the dirt.

This form of Ether mining is regarded as 'Proof-of-Work' mining. It is recognized as PoW (Proof-of-Work) since the node must demonstrate that it has completed the 'work' (validated the transactions) to obtain the Ether reward.

Buying Ethereum

Ether can be purchased from three different places:

- Brokerages, such as Coinbase, are cryptocurrency exchanges that charge a fee to buy and sell Ether. They are easy to use, but they can be very costly. They let you buy Ether with your fiat currency (USD, EUR, etc.) via credit/debit card or bank transfer. Cex.io, for example, uses an intermediary to bind buyers and sellers in an exchange (Cex). Traders use this to exchange one crypto for another. Buying Ether with Bitcoin, for instance, or selling NEO for Litecoin.

- LocalEthereum and other P2P platforms enable buyers and sellers to contact one another directly to bargain rates. Since you're trading directly with somebody, you don't know. This choice is riskier than the others. There is no mediator because there are no taxes, and you can pay with cash.

- Another great choice is to buy Ether coins through Simplex, a fintech company dedicated to ensuring full transaction security and fluidity. You'd also be able to purchase Ether with fiat currency, such as a credit or debit card, in this case.

Understanding the Smart Contract

Simply put, a "smart contract" is a protocol that runs on Ethereum's blockchain network. It's a set of code (its functions) and data (its state) that lives on the Ethereum blockchain network at a specific address.

How it Works

Let's begin by looking at how a smart contract could be applied. Let's assume Paul is interested in purchasing Peter's house. A smart contract is used to create this agreement on the Ethereum network. An arrangement between Paul and Peter is included in this smart contract.

The agreement would read something like this: "When John pays Mike 300 Ether, Then John receives possession of the house." This smart contract agreement can't be reversed once it's been set up, so John may feel comfortable paying Mike 300 Ether for the house.

Mike and John would have to pay a lot of money to an intermediary firm if they didn't use a smart contract in this case. The bank, a lawyer, and a real estate broker are among those options involved.

Isn't it fantastic? There will be no more fees and no more waiting for the agreement to be processed by a lawyer and broker! This is only one of the possible applications for a smart contract. More is abound in the world of NFTs.

When the agreement's terms are met, smart contracts are typically implemented. This eliminates the need for an intermediary such as a bank, broker, or government.

Digital Asset

So, to begin with, what exactly are digital assets? A digital asset is defined as "any digital item owned by an organization or entity, such as text, graphics, audio, video, animations, media, files, software, etc. Most people think of digital assets as just images and videos, but as time has gone by, we've begun to include other future collectibles in our definition, such as antiques, cars, and watches.

Any single item has three main elements that render it a digital asset. A digital asset must:

- Be a digital file
- Offer value to the individual or company
- Be searchable and discoverable (basically with metadata).

Chapter 3:
NEW NFT INVESTMENTS

NFT & Real Estate

How To Buy Virtual Land

Explore one of cryptocurrency's biggest movements in this chapter, and discover how to acquire virtual land, real estate, and other NFTs with the help of OpenSea and MetaMask.

Blockchain Property

NFTs are now used to build the large bulk of virtual land and related digital items on the Ethereum network. Owners of NFTs can have full control, actual ownership, and a secure manner of trading with others by utilizing this technology. NFTs and the assets they reflect, like any crypto, are held and saved in a 'wallet,' the most popular of which is MetaMask, a browser-based Ethereum wallet.

Buying Directly vs. Using a Marketplace

Individuals can acquire assets directly from several of the NFT projects' platforms. In 99 percent of circumstances, this is a completely appropriate method of purchasing digital assets, provided that the creator has not previously sold out and you are convinced that the platform is authentic and trustworthy.

Generally, we suggest using a peer-to-peer marketplace, of which there are many currently. OpenSea is our first pick, as it is by far the largest NFT marketplace. With all main NFTs listed on the marketplace, OpenSea has the largest trading volume and arguably the largest asset selection.

Using a reputable marketplace enables you to assess the level of interest in the asset, confirm that it is legitimate, and guarantee that you are paying the correct market price for the NFT.

Buying Your First NFT

Once you've completed your homework and are ready to buy the asset, there are a few things you need to do first. The procedure is generally easier than it appears, thanks to marketplaces like OpenSea.

After you've performed this job and written down your "Seed phrase" at least twice, you'll have to establish a suitable wallet (as stated earlier, we highly recommend MetaMask). You must deposit the necessary amounts into the wallet, almost always Ethereum (ETH) or another Ethereum-based crypto, like (MANA) in Decentraland. This stage entails using a platform like Coinbase to transform 'conventional money' into cryptocurrency. The cryptocurrency is subsequently sent to your Metamask wallet. You can also change fiat to cryptocurrency straight using Metamask, but you should first evaluate fees and determine which option is right for you.

Now that you have the necessary money, the remaining is a cake. There's no need to create an account; simply connect to the Marketplace (OpenSea) with your MetaMask wallet. When you find an NFT you wish to buy, just click buy or make an offer, and the remainder of the transaction will be automated, with OpenSea depositing the money into the seller's wallet and the NFT straight into your wallet. Then y you'll be able to control your asset right from your wallet or marketplace.

Selling you Real Estate NFT

Selling an NFT is essentially the same as buying one but in the opposite direction. Log in to the marketplace with the asset in your wallet, go to the asset, pick whether you like to advertise it for a set price or auction it off, and then select the desired price. Suppose a different user decides to buy the asset, the procedure will be entirely automated. The NFT will be sent to the prospective owner's wallet, while the money will be sent to your wallet. You may then retain the cryptocurrency in your wallet until you need it, or you may use a service like Coinbase to change it into fiat currency.

NFT & Mainstream Art

While art in the form of NFTs has been in the mainstream in recent months, the conventional art business has handled the market with care, with the exclusion of large auction houses and a few high-profile artists.

What is the true scale of the NFT art mainstream, notwithstanding the hype? How much of a stumbling block will it be? What role, if any, should conventional industry players play in the ultimate growth of the industry?

ArtTactic, a London-based study and advising firm, published a report that looked into the worldwide NFT art industry to answer these issues and look far beyond recent.

In an interview with Penta, Anders Petterson, owner and managing director of ArtTactic, said, "The recent surge of the NFT market, but lack of research and information, provided us with a chance to begin covering this area from the start, and to be able to follow and track its growth as we go forward." According to Petterson it's just as difficult to describe what makes "NFT art" as it is to describe what is and isn't art.

Based on this report, there are two broad types of NFT art platforms: open, non-curated platforms like OpenSea, and curated platforms like Nifty Gateway and SuperRare. Nifty Gateway released 3,009 NFTs with over 145,600 copies created for sale between February 2020 and April 2021, reflecting digital artworks by 272 artists. According to the report, the NFTs generated a sum of US$305 million.

In the main market, total sales were robust, with slightly over 139,000 copies purchased, marking a 95.5 percent total sale rate. The average cost was $1,228 USD. According to the report, the secondary market's total sales are nearly half that of the main market, but the average sales price is greater, at $1,938 per NFT.

According to the report, art has a market share of roughly 11% of the whole NFT market, based on sales.

The volume of the NFT art market is still insignificant when compared with the conventional art market. According to the annual Art Market Report from Art Basel and UBS, the traditional art market amounted to us$50.1 billion in 2020, with internet sales amounting to US$12.4 billion.

How Would Conventional Players Adapt

According to Petterson, the junction of art and technology is here to remain, and conventional art industry participants should accept the movement and join the NFT market's future growth.

"The NFT art market is really exciting because it provides new options for artists to build new markets and monetization

methods, as well as a new and appealing ownership m[...]
collectors," adds Petterson.

Mike Winkelmann, also known as Beeple, is the mos[...]
successful NFT artist, with a total of US$142.7 million in sales.
According to the article, which cites statistics from
Cryptoart.io, Pak comes in second with US$42 million in sales,
followed by Hackatao with US$21.6 million in sales. Leading
auction houses such as Christie's, Sotheby's, and Phillips
rapidly realized the potential of adopting NFTs, both in terms
of publicity and as a tool to help renew their aging client base.
"They've established themselves as a link between 'old' and
'new' art value systems. "This may be a road to pursue other
players in the art market," Petterson says.

NFT & Emerging Artists

Best Way to Succeed in the NFTs Market as Emerging Artist

An artist needs two things to succeed in NFTs: acumen and an
audience. Aside from mastering their skill, successful crypto
artists invest time growing their fan base and teaching
themselves on often complex crypto and blockchain protocols,
such as preventing fraud. Beeple had been polishing his digital
art abilities for nearly a decade before his first NFT sale,
notwithstanding his instantaneous popularity. Everyday—The
First 5,000 Days, his $69.3 million collage, is a collection of

activities, which he's been doing and

ꞌdel for

ꞌ.

ꞌwner of Nifty Gateway and collector of ...ι, says it all comes down to talent. He ₚₗₐins, "I believe being an artist is very much its skillset." "It necessitates going outside the box and doing something that is unlike anything else you've seen before in a way that grabs your attention. "Successful technical artists" are those who have achieved success.

Judging aesthetic excellence is highly subjective. It enables you to have an organization like Christie's to back you up when you control the millions that Beeple did. Mike Steib, the CEO of the art marketplace Artsy, claims that the NFT market isn't the open platform that many people assume it to be. "Can you tell me who sold Beelple? He claims that the procedure was not democratic. "Beeple was sold by Christie's, the world's biggest gatekeeper in the art industry.

Before Entering Into NFTs, Here Are a few Things Artists Should Know (and Do)

- **Understand NFTs**

The connection between the NFT marketplace, the artist, and the buyer must be understood: who owns what?

The artist created the piece, and he or she owns the copyright to it (given that they really made the piece). The buyer obtains a blockchain-supported ownership document that lists every former owner.

A service fee (similar to a commission) is normally charged by the NFT platform, which the seller may include in the sales price.

- **Pick the finest platform for creating and selling your artwork**

NFT markets' "do-it-yourself" procedure allows artists to sell cryptocurrency-art without the help of art middlemen or gallery. It's easy to get stuck with over 50 platforms to create and trade NFTs. Many minting networks also function as marketplaces, although not all of them are designed equally and follow varying business models. Certain platforms (e.g., Nifty Gateway, Knoworigin, Foundation, SuperRare) are curated and invite-only, while others demand user identification before participating in trades (e.g., Rarible, Foundation).

- **Security: Keep your information secure**

Look for two-factor verification when selecting a cryptocurrency wallet, keep your wallet address (analogous to a debit card number) and seed phrase (analogous to a password) secure, and get into the routine of using a VPN anytime trading cryptos. Artists must also check which wallets the NFT marketplace accepts (e.g., Foundation only uses MetaMask).

- **Be aware of copyright issues**

Copyright is a cornerstone of property rights, and artists ought to be aware of how and when to use it, particularly in the case of NFTs. Authors of creative visual, graphic, or sculptural pieces have the exclusive right to replicate and distribute versions of their work and the right to produce derivative works under the Copyright Act of 1976.

- **Make an informed business decision**

Changing one's artistic practice to cryptocurrency art should be approached as a business decision akin to selecting an art dealer or gallery. The cryptocurrency art industry is presently worth around $445 million, with Nifty Gateway leading the way in sales volume. Because the competition is severe, it's critical to comprehend the lingo, choose the best platform, and seek assistance from informed specialists. Expect this to be a slow and constant source of income; it's preferable not to set aside earnings from the sale of crypto art to pay rent. In this respect, it is similar to the "old" art market.

NFT Disruption Marketplaces

- Art

This is, without a doubt, a large industry. When NFTs are tied to digital art, it becomes possible to 'own' and trade it.

Here, ownership refers to the NFT that symbolizes the artwork. The artwork itself may be a single copy or a series of copies that the artist chooses to 'create.' Each artist selling art as NFTs for 6-7 digits has generated over $150 million in sales volume in the art sector solely!

- Virtual Land

You may own virtual land as NFTs with platforms such as Decentraland, The Sandbox, Cryptovoxels, Somnium Space, and Axie Infinity!

Because hundreds of people own land and may construct anything they like, from fitness centers to art galleries, the world can take on its shape, and you may sell your land afterward if the land near you improves in value!

- Game-related items

Consider your skins, firearms, armor, pets, and characters to be non-functional tokens (NFTs) that you may upgrade and sell. Perhaps you have a very rare item, and as the user base develops, more people desire it.

People invest billions in the gaming industry, even though putting money into games is typically deemed "sunk money." Why shouldn't they invest it if they're obtaining an NFT for all the time they've spent to improve and sell on a marketplace?

- Trading Card Game (TCG) - More games

Buying and selling Card games, in particular, appear to be a perfect fit, given the purpose of card games is to compete against others and trade.

Pokemon, Hearthstone, YuGiOh, and Magic: the Gathering is all quite famous in this sense, with millions of collectors and gamers worldwide. We've all seen how many rare cards like Charizard can fetch in the real world.

Splinterlands and Gods Unchained are leading the charge!

- Collectibles are number five

The collectibles market is enormous. Cryptopunks have sold for $1 million or more, and crypto kitties have gone viral. Even in the digital age, the sense of ownership and the need to possess something famous appears to be alive and strong.

- Sports Collectibles

With renowned businesses and players involved, NBA Top Shot has surpassed $100 million in sales. These NFTs aren't just for collecting; they may also be used in a variety of activities. In fact, these NFTs may be used to create an entire environment of sports games!

- Domain names

Domain names ending in.eth and.crypto are in high demand. Individuals utilize them to modify their payment addresses, pay directly using a Twitter handle, and, ultimately, host websites. Whatever can be owned can be an NFT, so why not domain names?

- NFT Marketplaces

Because NFTs are decentralized or "open," anybody can create a marketplace to begin buying and selling them. Nearly every NFT project has traded millions of NFTs through Opensea!

- DeFi-Decentralized Finance

Certain projects, such as Bondly, enable you to use your NFT to trade cryptocurrency for no cost. Isn't it amazing?

NFTs can and will be utilized in a variety of blockchain-based decentralized financial applications.

- Digi-physical products

Is there a physical aspect that also includes an NFT? Both are distinct assets. In real life, Metafactory, for instance, sells bespoke sweatshirts that come with an NFT that you can use in Cryptovoxels! The Headspace does this as well, and some of their NFTs may be seen in Decentraland.

Nifty Gateway's recent Fewocious and RTFKT studios drop sold nearly $3 million in shoes and NFTs, with NFT holders entitled to claim a set of Fewocious art shoes! And then there's Crypto Kaiju, the originals in the space who make Vinyl toys out of NFTs.

- Virtual scenes

NFTs can be used to create entire virtual buildings and games! Metazone is a fantastic initiative that enables Decentraland landowners to purchase and deploy games, structures, and enhancements on their land.

Consider the rental market if you'd like to host a gathering on your land but don't want to spend $4000 on development. Why not rent one for the weekend for $200? As the virtual area on blockchain expands, this model's potential is enormous.

- Fractionalize/shared ownership

Are you unable to purchase the NFT of your dreams?

Why not buy a fraction of the item? NFTX and Niftex are fascinating projects that enable you to share your NFT into thousands of ERC20 tokens, enabling others to own and exchange them on a marketplace.

- Insurance policies/contracts

Yes, it is correct. NFTs can be used to own complete insurance policies or financial services contracts. In fact, as Gabby discovered with Yearn Finance, you may become a digital insurance broker by structuring insurance and offering it as NFTs.

- Virtual cars

Why can't we have virtual cars, planes, and ships as NFTs in a virtual space?

Many have auctioned virtual cars for hundreds of ETH, and as blockchain virtual spaces evolve, so will the need for sophisticated modes of transportation and exploration. This area has been investigated by CryptoMotors, F1 Delta Time, and Battle Racers.

- Gold Backed NFTs

The Bullionix project enables you to establish a DGX-backed NFT. Because one DGX token is backed by one gram of gold, the NFT is essentially backed or fixed to its created DGX/gold value. Isn't that amazing?

Imagine winning gold medals at tournaments as NFTs supported by golds. This is the case at Decentraland's moonshot competition, which attracted 20+ teams to compete in a virtual football game!

Chapter 4:
FUTURE COLLECTIBLES

The Basics of Collectibles

Collectibles are goods that can be bought or sold for a considerably higher price than they were originally worth. If they're in short supply, they can be far more valuable. However, the state of the goods has a significant impact on the amount you can earn from them. You'll be likely to earn more for your collectible if it's in good condition. There's a reasonable risk you won't receive anything at all if it's degraded.

Bear in mind, however, that collectibles aren't as widespread as you might expect, and they might not be as good an asset as you assume. After all, it's a famously volatile market, not to say one that's both costly and vast. From stamps to plush animals, individuals collect a wide range of goods. And amassing a significant collection takes time.

Let's imagine you've done your homework on what's hot right now and are considering what might make you money in the long term. You intend to purchase goods at face value today and observe their value rise dramatically. However, this might take so many years.

It's simple to keep track of what's hot on the internet right now. Look at what's hot on eBay (EBAY). You can equally receive help with putting your own products on the market. It's important to remember that certain collectibles only hold their value if they're preserved in their initial condition. "New in Box" (NIB) is defined as "a collectible that is new, in its box, and has never been removed from its initial packaging," according to eBay." "Mint in the Box" "(MIB) contrarily denotes that the goods are "in mint state and in its original, unsealed box."

The Future of Collectibles

Whether it's because sentimental collectors in their 30s and 40s are returning to the pastime they enjoyed as kids, investors are looking for inflation-hedged items after more than $20 trillion in world economic boost was distributed in 2020, or the COVID-19 impact, the outcome is evident:

The collectible market is booming. Ken Goldin launched Goldin Auctions in 2012, a platform for collectibles and trading cards (like Sotheby's for sports) that made $800,000 in its first year. On the other hand, Goldin Auctions saw $27 million in auction traffic in 2019, only seven years after its debut, representing a 65 percent annual growth rate.

Goldin Auctions witnessed more than $100 million in sale activity last year, a 270 percent increase year over year, as investors rushed to the item class for numerous reasons. They sold over 1,000 products for $33 million in January this year alone. That's more than they sold in the entire year of 2019, putting them on track to hit $200 million in revenue this year, which would be more than double their previous high of $100 million in 2020.

To put it another way, the demand has been out of this world. It's time to put your money where your mouth is. Together with an outstanding roster of celebrity investors from the sports, journalism, and entertainment industries, TCG confirmed that they are putting $40 million in Goldin Auctions.

Ken Goldin will become executive chairman as a contract component, while Ross Hoffman, who previously worked at Twitter, Google, and Headspace, will take over as CEO.

What's my opinion on the Investment? It's only the start. When we speak of sports trading cards and general collectibles as a real alternative asset class, the usual talking points concentrate around annual returns that outperform the S& P 500, which is true (at 270 percent versus 160 percent since January 2008).

All of this is fantastic, but let's be frank: the extreme investment in sports trading cards and memorabilia entails far more than historical returns. Young people, on the other hand, do not desire a 60/40 stock/bond portfolio. Consumers don't want a yield stock portfolio, and the GameStop debacle has told us that they can't trust Wall Street.

They would like to invest in the long-term, which they say includes trading cards, collectibles, cryptos, NFTs, digital art, and more, regardless you agree with them or not. It doesn't actually matter if you think those things are legit investment options or not. A host of active investors believe it because they have more access to information, technology, and data than they have ever had before. That is what counts in the end.

Persistent client interest was the first step in making collectibles a future sustainable alternative asset class. That is in our possession. Step two now involves venture capital investment in additional services that will boost customer experience and decrease market barriers, resulting in faster overall industry development.

That's presently happening as a spoiler alert. One example is TCG's $40 million investment in Goldin Auctions to expand its technology, logistics, and audience development. Other options comprise venture-supported firms such as Collectable, Rally Rd., and OTIS, which enable you to acquire a fractional part of valuable collectibles or innovative portfolio management tools such as ALT.

Remember that earlier in the year, Wall Street giants Steve Cohen and Dan Sundheim joined forces with businessman and sports card collector Nat Turner to purchase Collectors Universe, the leading authenticity and grading services firm, for $850 million.

That is, without a doubt, significant. Finally, collectibles provide an emotional connection and sense of community that few other things can match.

Price fluctuation will ultimately level off, but you should not wager against a group asset with a strong emotional connection, as its emotional connection will determine that asset's future worth. Supply and demand economics will prevail, as it has in the past. Tomorrow's winners are already aware of it. That translates to more organizational investment, which seems to be on the horizon if you look carefully.

How to Invest in Collectibles

So, rather than stocks and bonds, you have some spare money and want to put it in something different? The possibilities are unlimited. However, when we speak of interesting investments, collectibles are hard to top!

However, like with any investment, there is uncertainty. Before committing funds to any investment, you should definitely seek advice from a professional. With that in mind, here are some general recommendations from Neat Stuff Collectibles to help you get started investing in collectibles:

- **Be aware of your timeline**

Understanding how long you intend to keep a collection as an investment before selling it will help you establish an acceptable price to pay for it and set your revenue target. For instance, if you get a great offer on a collectible, you might like to sell it quickly. If you locate a truly rare collectible at a reasonable price, you may wish to keep it for a long period and then sell it after its value has increased significantly.

- **Buy low and sell high**

Investing in collectibles is all about buying low and selling high. Although it's easy to overlook the fundamentals when attempting to keep track of everything, it may appear straightforward. It's also easier to make reasonable buying and selling decisions if you remember the full procedure from start to finish!

- **Begin small**

Of course, starting a new pastime, particularly one that might be financially profitable, is thrilling! However, don't get too connected too soon. That's a surefire way to get burnt out and feel disappointed. Rather, begin little and gradually. This can help you generate excitement for your next transaction while also reducing risk as you learn the technique and, eventually, make mistakes.

- **Handle the Collectibles appropriately**

Once you've purchased a collectible and it's in your control, don't allow its value to plummet unduly due to improper storage practices. Increase the value of your collectibles by carefully keeping them. This is a terrific strategy to increase the value of your collectibles should you intend to keep them for a long period. Keep your unique goods in immaculate shape and minimize damage as much as possible. They will be in far better shape than analogous items on the market, rendering yours more desirable!

- **Find collectibles that catch your interest**

Last but not least, buy collectibles that pique your interest! It's critical to be enthusiastic and thrilled about your products. You'll remain interested and creative. Just remember to keep your emotions out of it while deciding on a fair price for purchasing and selling!

10 Proven Strategies for Making Money Investing in Collectibles

1. Invest exclusively in collectibles for which you have a thorough understanding of the market: It has been discovered that investing money in collectibles is exceedingly challenging if you do not understand that specific form of collectible. Let's imagine you walk into a store or a kiosk that sells the types of collectibles you're looking to buy. Could you name the price for much of what was on display there if that seller took out the prices from all the items they were selling? If you can't accomplish that, you probably shouldn't invest in collectibles in the long run.

2. Keep up with any collectibles market you're interested in: If you don't keep up with the market you're interested in, you can miss out on a price decrease. So it's not a great idea to engage in a pastime if you're not engaged sufficiently in it to devote some time every week – or at the very minimum, every month – to stay up to date with the development. It's no different from trading individual stocks: if you're not staying up to date with the industry, you're making a mistake by buying its shares.

3. Get your collectibles by bargain hunting: Buying from dealers is a bad investment as the prices they have on

products are rarely cheap. Rather, seek out unusual locations to round out your collection. Yard sales, as well as Goodwill and vintage stores, should be frequented. You may come across other products you are not fascinated with when bargain hunting, but you should buy them and sell them for a fast buck.

4. Usually, try to see products in person if possible: It is always good to see the products you wish to buy in person. You'll be able to discover forgeries and products with serious faults if you inspect the objects in person. Most prestigious auctions include pre-auction viewings during which you can question the vendor. Otherwise, only do business with people you know and trust.

5. Make a budget and adhere to it: Spend as much as you can. However, buy the best you can with what you have. Key elements such as quality, uniqueness, and authenticity play a role here.

6. Keep your treasures safe: it's not a good idea to leave your collectibles unattended. You should keep them in a safe place with little chance of theft. If you invest in extremely rare objects, a safe deposit box at a bank branch is the best solution for many people.

7. If at all feasible, have your most precious objects adequately graded. Professional grading entails having an outside agency evaluate the item's provenance and state. They will frequently seal the object to prevent it

from being altered. Grading will not reduce the worth of your object, but it will almost probably boost it. Any object with a value of $500 or more is typically worth the cost of skilled grading. For things of lower value, the cost of grading can account for a significant portion of the item's value, necessitating a significant price increase to compensate.

8. Avoid the intermediary: Anytime possible, buy directly from the source and avoid the intermediary. You may be able to purchase directly from the artist in some situations. For instance, purchase pottery directly from artisans. In the long run, this will save you a lot of money.

9. Get a buyback warranty: If possible, get a formal warranty from the seller that if you decide to sell, they will repurchase the product from you for at least the very same price you paid or more within five years. This is a smart technique to avoid being tied to an object for the long - term if you wouldn't want to be.

10. Diversify your investments: Don't put all of your money into collectibles; variety is king. Putting all of your money in stocks isn't a good idea. It's counterintuitive to keep all of your money in cash. It's not a good idea to put all of your money into real estate. It's also not a good idea to put all of your money into collectibles. Diversity rules the world. You don't want to go

bankrupt if the collection market collapses. Collectibles are non-essential products, whether you like them or not, and customers can be capricious. If your hobbies change, your set's worth could plummet suddenly, which is something you don't want to risk.

Things to Buy That Could Soon Be Collectibles

Here are some suggestions for identifying collectibles that may—and this is the key word—increase in value in the future.

- **Memorabilia from sports**

If you're a sports lover, you might be interested in sports memorabilia. You may have grabbed a fly ball or, better still, received the game ball just after Super Bowl—and had it autographed. You might be able to cash in if that's the case.

However, a spike in fraudulent autographs has put a damper on this once-profitable industry. Follow this trick to ensure the legitimacy of an autographed product: when you have your sports star autograph a ball or other item, have somebody take a picture of you with the player as they hold the pen. With such visual proof, no one can reject the autograph.

- **Toys**

Let's imagine you've previously gone through your house looking for any untouched toys you could have tucked away, like those original Star Wars miniatures your son scoffed at a century ago. Consider what's hot in toys right now that you might buy at face value. Toys that are related to films are usually a tremendous hit. Besides, these aren't large investments.

Disney collectibles have long been popular. Limited-edition "Frozen" dolls, perhaps? Oh my, it's too late. Several have already been listed on eBay, with one going for $2,999.99. No one would have expected the worldwide success of "Frozen." But take a look at what Disney has planned. "Raya and the Last Dragon" is being produced by the studio. The 59th animated movie from Disney is a fantasy picture about a little girl called Raya who embarks on a quest to discover the world's last dragon. Though this won't be available till March 12, 2021, there's still time to note in your diary so you can get your hands on those dolls as soon as they're available.

After you've purchased a few dolls, store them safely in their original packaging and examine their value periodically over the next couple of years. They have the potential to become the next major Disney collectible.

- **Emerging Photographers**

In recent times, collectors have struck it rich in the realm of art photography. In 2007, three US collectors discovered a massive collection of prints and negatives by Vivian Maier, a then-anonymous street photographer who worked from the 1950s until the 1970s. When one of the collectors, John

Maloof, posted a few of the images on his blog in 2009, the world soon recognized Maier's enormous talent. Her work has been included in various books and documentaries ever since, with prints beginning at $4,500.

Mike Japp, an appraiser, shares a related story about Frank Worth, a photographer. When he was granted access to movie sets, Worth took candid shots of the stars. Images of a somber James Dean slumped in a lawn chair behind a wire fence on the set of "Giant," which first appeared just over the years back, retail for roughly $5,200.

How do you track down an emerging photographer? Local galleries and student art displays should be visited. You can equally look for information on the internet. There is also an "Emerging Photographer" magazine. Follow your intuition and acquire art you enjoy and would like to hang on your walls, even if it isn't appreciated. Good art can help to lift one's emotions.

The Future of Electronics

It should come as no surprise that there is a demand for old technological items. An outdated system that you once struggled to unload may suddenly be worth three times its initial cost and advertised on eBay as a "wonderful talking piece." Collectors share ideas on sites like VintageComputer.com.

The most costly electronic devices, like the Apple I, are the first of their kind. One is currently for sale on eBay for $1.5 million. A 1976 Apple I system sold for $671,400.11 at auction in Cologne, Germany, in 2013.

Old electronics aren't always worth a lot of money. A 1984 Authentic Apple Macintosh 128k, for instance, recently sold for $2,749 on eBay. Prices for "NIB" products, on the other hand, are skyrocketing. A 20 GB Apple iPod classic 2nd Generation fresh in its factory-sealed box is sold for $29,999.99 and characterized as "COLLECTORS RARE VINTAGE NEW."

Who knows how much an unopened original iPad will be worth in 2025? Keep an eye out for the next revolutionary electrical gadget to hit the market and seize it. Is there an Apple Watch? Perhaps not. But there's going to be something spectacular in the near future.

Things to Collect for The Future

Vintage Fashion

Sites like Etsy and Depop are recording rising demand, no doubt fueled by the millennial climate-conscious. As an alternative to buying new, millennials have begun to collect low-cost one-of-a-kind items. Pieces from the late 1980s, early 1990s, and even the early 2000s have become very popular.

Memorabilia

Travel posters from the 1960s and 1970s are still famous, as are all items "Space" related (particularly anything connected to Star Wars and the early Star Trek series).

Pop memorabilia and pop-culture objects from the 1960s, 1970s, and 1980s are also in high demand, with antique cameras, vinyl albums, games, and movie posters all gaining popularity.

Vintage Engagement Rings

Having previously worked in an antique center, this is unsurprising. The ancient beauty and originality of an antique engagement ring are attracting more and more fashionable brides-to-be. Not only that, but we're all (hopefully) becoming more ecologically aware and realizing that you can get a lot more bang for your buck while also preserving the earth!

Victorian

No other category has experienced such a huge surge as Victorian-era things. Millennials, according to sources, have begun purchasing low-cost Victorian artifacts as an alternative to buying new, and again, with an eye on preserving the earth. Furniture and the more unusual ornamental pieces seem to be doing fairly well.

So, folks, you can clearly see what will unfold in the nearest future. The mid-century modern craze will eventually pave the way to the old brown antique furniture that you can get cheaply right now! Investing in it now could prove to be a wise decision!

China Antiques

Both purchasing and selling remain extremely strong in this area, especially in the foreign market. Bronze figurines and porcelain artifacts from dynasties like the Ch'ing have recently sold for record sums. Almost everything that can be proven to have a link to china's history continues to sell briskly.

Silver and gold

We saw a historical gold price last year as a result of international affairs. With the continuous risk associated with the financial markets, individuals are looking to put their funds in more secured items, and gold and silver appear to be attractive choices.

Coins

One of the most valuable collector objects is coins. The scarcity of the coins and the material they are composed of, particularly gold or silver, will determine how much they grow in value and can be traded for. Coin collecting is something that can be done for a long time. Anyone interested in starting a coin collection should seek help from professionals and seasoned collectors, as there is a lot to learn to safeguard one's investment.

Coin collecting in the US alone is worth billions of dollars per year, according to Coin Trackers. Coin collecting may not yield immediate profits, but it can accumulate and store large money. Gold coins, according to the study, are ideal for collecting.

If one is serious about investing in gold, US Gold suggests allocating 10 to 30% of its investment. Gold is more than just an asset; it is genuine money that is usually preferable to cash. According to the Huffington Post, a gold coin struck in the United States in 1933 was sold for $7.2 million in 2002.

Art and artifacts

Due to their cultural significance, certain collectibles are worth millions of dollars. Works by Pablo Picasso, for instance, are regarded as the blue chips of the art industry According to The Guardian, Picasso's "Women of Algiers" went for $179 million in 2015 at Christie's in New York. It was created in the early to mid-1950s as one of a sequence of pieces by the artist.

Investing in art will necessitate a detailed understanding of art history and how various works have been valued on the market. If the collector isn't well-versed in this area, professional assistance will be required.

Culture

Those who desire to recreate their childhood experiences gather comic books, antique toys, and other mementos from the past. If these antiques are kept properly, they can be worth thousands of dollars. More modern instances of pop culture, such as the comic Amazing Spider-Man #1 and Superman's debut in Action Comics #1, have joined the list of valued collectibles such as stamps and baseball cards.

Wine

If you can keep yourself from popping the corks, wine can be an excellent long-term investment, but you must be very selective about which wines you buy. Hoarding a collection of the best wines brewed by the premier chateaux of Bordeaux and then selling them for an enormous profit has provided investors with fair earnings in the past.

Nevertheless, because investing in wine is a complicated subject, you should spend time learning about it before determining whether or not to participate in it. The golden rule applies to any alternative investment: simply risk what you can afford to lose.

Automobiles

The great news is that the historic automobile market has been booming for some years. It's a tangible object you keep in your carport, and you can't put a price on the enjoyment you get from using it. Also, if you buy wisely and do not require extensive repairs, you may appreciate it in two or three years.

Automobiles appreciate for some reasons. It's sometimes a manufacturer's fantastic new automobiles that reinvigorate attention in their forebears, while other times it's a designer's anniversary that propels it to popularity.

Stamps

One of the most popular collections is a stamp collection. It can be a profitable business if you choose your stamps carefully, as some unusual ones can go for millions of dollars. The most valuable stamps have yielded annual average returns of roughly 9.7%, with collectors driving the prices.

Daily, stamp collectors trade millions of dollars worth of stamps. Since they do not correspond substantially with any other asset categories, stamps can be a smart way to diversify your investments. The objective is to find a reliable dealer who can help you navigate the stamp collecting and selling procedure.

Chapter 5:
ASSET CATEGORIES

- Comic Books

Comic books are still a common collector's item, and the older and scarce your comic book is, the more valuable it is. However, just because your comic book collection has some rare and old editions doesn't mean it's worth a million dollars. When purchasing, selling, or trading comic books, you must consider extra considerations. For instance, you should study the marketability of your comic book. The value of comics with famous covers as well as first debuts is usually higher.

Most Expensive Comic Books

For example, in 2014, a 1938 issue of Action Comics #1 sold on eBay for $3.21 million. When it initially came out, Action Comics #1 cost ten cents and included the first appearance of Superman. In addition to being antique, the comic book is extremely uncommon, with just about 100 copies known to exist. Any first edition of a comic book series, in essence, may be extremely valuable.

- Coins

Coin collectors have a rewarding occupation. Coins might be one of the best things to collect for investment, depending on their scarcity and quality.

Figure out how much your coins are worth before selling or auctioning them off if you have a coin collection that you believe contains historical rarities. You can also have your coins graded by going to the Professional Coin Grading Service website.

Most Expensive Coins

The rare 1894-S Barber dime normally sells for more than $1 million, although it has sold for more than $2 million in private transactions. An 1894-S Barber, for example, sold for $1.99 million in 2016 at an auction in Tampa, Florida.

- Stamps

Stamps are yet another popular collectible, and rare stamps are among the finest opportunities to earn money from stamp collecting. Prepare your stamp collection if you wish to sell any of your expensive stamps for cash. If your collection is structured, it will likely sell for higher money.

Most Expensive Stamps

Take the "Inverted Jenny" stamp, for example. Only 100 exist, and one with a catalog value of $1.6 million was auctioned off in 2016. The stamp didn't actually sell for that much, but a private bidder paid $1.17 million for it. The stamp was originally priced at 24 cents, which is a fantastic return on the investment.

The 1867 Benjamin Franklin stamp is another example of a high-valued stamp. Just two specimens are known to exist, making the stamp worth $935,000. Another instance is the 1869 stamp of the Declaration of Independence.

- Dolls

You could be sitting on a jackpot of collectibles if you've been collecting collectible dolls for years, perhaps because you want to pass them on. Although selling one toy for $1 million or more may be difficult, selling several could help you get close. Your return could be much greater if you have a properly managed collection of dolls.

Most Expensive Dolls

Cabbage Patch Kids may generate a lot of interest — and money. There are multiple postings on eBay for Cabbage Patch dolls from the 1970s and 1980s, some of which are priced for as much as $10,000. Barbie is another popular collectible; the 1959 version may fetch hundreds of dollars on eBay.

- Action Figures

The field of collectible action figures is vast and varied. These collectibles can win you a significant gain, ranging from old models with their lovely, hand-painted pieces to more current ones that are simply unique. When it comes to collecting, some collectors are willing to pay more than what they believe something is worth adding to their personal collection. After all, the most valuable dolls have been practically neglected and are in excellent shape.

Most Expensive Action Figures

In 2003, a private sale fetched $200,000 for the 1963 G.I. Joe. Supergirl and Wonder Woman, among other 1960s Ideal Comics superheroines, can bring a huge amount of money. A quick search on eBay for the phrase "action figure" will turn up hundreds of dollars worth of action figures and action figure collections. These action figures you uncovered at estate sales or in the home of an elderly family member might be worth a lot more than you think.

- Board Games

Selling a single board game for $1 million or more may be difficult. In 2011, a craftsman produced a gold-plated Monopoly board and set that cost more than $2 million.

Purchasing the set would undoubtedly be a luxury only the ultra-wealthy could afford.

Even if you don't have $2 million worth of board game gathering dust in your garage or attic, a sizable collection of old board games can quickly build up.

Most Expensive Board Games

Monopoly sets aren't the only valuable board games. A fast search on eBay will turn up several board game sets that are valued at $1,000 or more. A 1974 jubilee edition of Monopoly, for instance, is offered for slightly under $2,500.

- Trading cards

Baseball cards are frequently sought after memorabilia. If any of the cards in your collection are rare, you might be in fortune. Seven T206 Ty Cobb baseball cards found in the garbage in March 2016 made headlines as they were valued at around $1 million – each card was worth approximately $150,000.

Most Expensive Trading Cards

In 2016, Goldin Auctions sold a 1909-11 T206 Honus Wagner baseball card for $3.12 million, making it the most valuable baseball card ever. The baseball card had already sold for $2.1 million on the internet three years beforehand. Just 200 of the card were ever manufactured.

Baseball cards aren't the only sort of trading cards that are valued. According to eBay postings, the first-edition collection of Yu-Gi-Oh! Legacy of Darkness cards in mint condition may fetch about a thousand dollars, and a rare Magic: The Gathering card sold for $166,100 in 2019.

- 'Star Wars' Collectibles

"Star Wars" is a cultural phenomenon with its own holiday, and licensed merchandise is in high demand. If you have some things from the original series in your "Star Wars" collection, you could have a great nest egg worth close to $1 million.

Most Expensive 'Star Wars' Collectibles

One fan received $505,202 for his 600-item "Star Wars" collection. Although, some goods were more valuable than others. A flawless multipack of seven "Star Wars" action figures from "The Empire Strikes Back," for instance, sold for well over $30,000, more than three times its estimated value. In addition, a Luke Skywalker toy that had been recalled went for $25,000 on eBay. Meanwhile, a Yak Face, a creature from "Return of the Jedi," sold only for $7,250, whereas an Anakin Skywalker figurine from "Return of the Jedi" went for only $3,000.

- Memorabilia

To make at least $1 million from a movie collectible, you must first acquire it, which may be tough given how valuable these objects are. Objects from cult films like "The Wizard of Oz" or those worn by celebrities who made an impact but died too young, like James Dean, will certainly bring so much money.

Most Expensive Memorabilia

For instance, the Cowardly Lion costume from "The Wizard of Oz" and the "Casablanca" piano sold for $3 million at Bonham's Turner Classic Movies auction and $3.4 million, respectively.

- Books

You could get some money from valuable books if you have first editions. Books can be costly for a variety of reasons and characteristics, including exclusivity and binding integrity. Do some research to discover if you have a treasure at your disposal before you discard your books or choose to rebind them.

The Most Expensive Books

"Harry Potter and the Philosopher's Stone" paperback original editions may fetch up to $45,000, whereas "Harry Potter and the Chamber of Secrets" may fetch around $7,000. If it's in excellent shape, the original edition of F. Scott Fitzgerald's classic "The Great Gatsby" may bring as much as $400,000.

- Other Toys

Action figures and vintage board games are valuable childhood relics, and having a few of the correct items in your old toy chest might be worth a lot of money. Consider toys like Teddy Ruxpin, Strawberry Shortcake, Transformers, and My Little Pony, which were all the vogue at the time. Get yours out if you still have it stashed away to see what it's worth.

Most Expensive Toys

For example, Lite-Brite, an illuminated artboard into which plastic pegs are inserted to create glowing art, may fetch over $100. Dolls from My Little Pony might fetch $900. Transformers from the 1980s can fetch up to $750, while a Teddy Ruxpin toy from 1985 can fetch hundreds of dollars.

- Sports Memorabilia

Collectible sports memorabilia owners can make a fortune with just one object. You could get a solid start toward a million-dollar nest egg if you're lucky, like the stadium fan who was gifted one of Tom Brady's infamous Deflategate balls used in the AFC Championship game in 2015. She got $44,000 for it at auction.

Most Expensive Sports Memorabilia

If you could somehow lay your hands on a Super Bowl ring, that's another beautiful example of how sports memorabilia can make you a lot of money. In 2015, the 1985 Super Bowl XX ring worn by William "Refrigerator" Perry sold for more than $200,000 at auction. Players' game gear, trade cards, and trophies can also bring in a lot of money.

- Wristwatches

With that classic watch you inherited or discovered at an estate sale, the vintage-watch-collecting market might fetch a nice deal. Just because you don't recognize the name doesn't imply it's not valuable. Although most people can identify Rolex and Patek Philippe, they may not be familiar with lesser-known yet expensive brands such Universal Geneve or Enicar.

Most Expensive Wristwatches

Chrono24, a Rolex Submariner Date, may be valued at $9,626. A search for Patek Phillippe Nautilus turns up on a page of watches with outlandish price tags, several of which cost between $30,000 and $500,000. To gain a more precise estimate of your watch's worth, enter its reference number into Chrono24's free, online evaluation service.

- Music Memorabilia

Getting a piece of music memorabilia from your favorite singer could be exciting, and if you chose to sell a series of such items, you could make a nice profit. According to Heritage Auctions, items linked with rock & roll, blues, and jazz stars have done exceptionally well in this category of collectibles. In fact, if you have musical memorabilia, an auction house is the best location to find out how much it is worth.

Most Expensive Music Memorabilia

According to Heritage Auctions, music artists and bands like Buddy Holly, the Beatles, the Rolling Stones, and Jim Morrison are excellent collectibles to trade. On Sept. 7, 1964, a Beatles press box show tickets for admittance to Maple Leaf Gardens in Toronto went for $3,500.

Even collections by newer artists who died unexpectedly or prematurely might be highly expensive. For instance, on the Heritage Auction site, a silk outfit owned and worn by reclusive and secretive artist Prince went for $10,000.

- Collectible Statues

Celebrities, cartoon characters, and superheroes are among the topics of collectible statues. The perfect state your piece is in, the greater value it will have, as with many collectible objects. Don't let the fact that your statue is a little battered prevent you from evaluating its worth. You might simply be sitting on a tiny fortune.

Most Expensive Collectible Statues

Sideshow statues sell exceptionally well on eBay, maybe because many of them are labeled as rare or unique first versions. On eBay, for instance, Sideshow's Thor Jane Foster statue went for nearly $800. The limited-edition Batman vs. Killer Croc statue from DC Direct sold for $410.

The moral of the story is that if you could get your hands on a unique edition statue when it first comes out, you may be able to sell it for a much greater price later.

- Art Prints

While you may believe that art prints are simply large-scale posters, you would be mistaken. Depending on the context and the creator, art prints have their marketplace and could even be expensive. According to Christie's, there are many distinct sorts of prints. However, the four most well-known are etching, lithography, screenprint, and woodcut.

A printing fraction is a number that appears on certain prints. The number of the specific print inside a print run appears at the top of the fraction. The number at the bottom indicates that print copies were printed during that print run. The overall number of prints produced determines the value of a print run. The less of them there are, the more precious they are.

Most Expensive Art Print

To generate income from your art, you don't have to own a Picasso or a Rembrandt print. There are a lot of other prints that are worth a fortune. A set of signed Norman Rockwell "Puppy Love" lithographs, for example, is sold on eBay for $19,999.99; a brief search on the site shows that Norman Rockwell prints sell for thousands of dollars.

Vintage Peter Max prints could be extremely valuable. A quick check on eBay saw prints going for as much as $16,000.

- Movie Posters

According to Collector's Weekly, if you own a historic movie poster from a picture published before the 1940s, you may be sitting on a jackpot. Some of these posters survive since they were utilized as marketing and were not kept by movie theater owners. Rather, they were directed to the next cinema presenting the film. In fact, it wasn't until 1977, when "Star Wars" was produced, that individuals began to take an interest in collecting movie posters.

Most Expensive Movie Posters

According to Heritage Auctions, if you like to sell your movie poster collection, an antique item from 1910 to 1950 is typically the most valuable. Famous horror and science-fiction films, including those starring Marilyn Monroe, James Dean, early Walt Disney cartoons, and Alfred Hitchcock, to mention a few, command high prices.

According to Collector's Weekly, posters from the 1950s showcasing movies such as "The War of the Worlds" and "The Day the Earth Stood Still" are desirable, and those themed on 1930s horror movies such as "Frankenstein" and "Dracula" could also fetch a good price.

- Medals and Badges

Medals and badges may be exchanged for cash in different ways. These objects are still worthwhile to look at, even though you'll need to acquire quite a collection to earn $1 million.

Original old sheriff's badges, firefighter and railroad badges, and vintage military medals can also be valued. Even some toy badges might be pretty valuable. Just ensure that whatever you acquire is genuine, as fakes are rampant, according to Collectors Weekly.

Most Expensive Medals and Badges

If you're a fan of the BBC tv series "Dr. Who," don't miss the toy vintage badges associated with the show. In London, four Dr. Who and Dalek badges from the 1960s went for a sum of over $2,300.

According to Collectors Weekly, Union items are more desirable than Confederate ones when it comes to Civil War military medals and badges. Furthermore, be aware that replicas are popular in this area. The first income tax was also made necessary by the Civil War.

- Video Game Collectibles

According to Time, even though vintage games are frequently released online, collectors still prefer the original editions. The better the state of the game, the greater the value. Another piece of advice is that games that were deemed unique editions are desirable and can be sold on eBay for a good price. Convert the video games that have been taking up space in your household into money.

Most Expensive Video Games

Naturally, if you own a sealed version of a collectible game, you can expect to receive more. On eBay, for instance, sealed versions of Nintendo's "Castlevania" fetch thousands of dollars. The same can be said for classic video games featuring Sonic the Hedgehog. You may get an estimate of how much your old video games are worth by searching on eBay or a reliable old video game website.

- Legos

Legos are, without a doubt, regarded toys. According to the corporation, the word Lego stems from the Danish words "leg godt," meaning "play well." Irrespective of the meaning of the brand's name, it requires its own category. Though Lego bricks are essential for building structures, they aren't particularly valuable on their own. However, if you have particular Lego sets, you could make a lot of money.

Most Expensive Legos

Like "Star Wars"-themed products, Legos are extremely collectible and frequently value more than what you spent for them. On eBay, Lego Millennium Falcon sets can go for hundreds of dollars or even more, with first-version sets fetching thousands of dollars.

If you have a Lego train set, you could be in business - old railroad sets may be very profitable. On eBay, an old mechanized train from 1966 is offered for $10,000. According to eBay, a sealed 1980 Diesel Freight Train might be worth more than $2,000 if it is in good condition.

Chapter 6:
ETHEREUM AND THE
FUTURE OF NFTs

A Novel Way for Artist and Creatives

Acc, ccording to digital designers, the introduction of NFTs will spark a surge of artistic creativity by allowing artists to sell avant-garde work directly to buyers. 3D artist Alexis Christodoulou told Dezeen, "We're absolutely at the frontier." "Now that you're in control, you have the opportunity to build something amazing."

Andrés Reisinger, who sold ten digital furniture works as NFTs, continued, "You can fully engage with the individuals that consume and admire your art." So, you don't need any middlemen like a brand or gallery as we've substituted these entities with code.

Non-fungible tokens (NFTs) have currently made headlines due to their application in the sale of virtual art, fashion, and even real estate. Andreas Wannerstedt, a motion graphics artist, feels that this will eventually encourage designers to develop more avant-garde work. "I believe that so many high-level artists and designers would try to shift away from commercial design and concentrate more on their work," he told Dezeen.

"This would take a little time before the public realizes the actual power of NFTs, but the ability to generate a distinctive digital file offers a lot of opportunities, and what we are experiencing now is simply the start."

"Many formats have not yet been tested" Non-fungible tokens (NFTs) are digital proofs of legitimacy and ownership that can be granted to digital assets like videos, jpegs, and gifs. Like a bitcoin transaction, every token is separately registered or created on a blockchain network, enabling the related asset to be purchased, sold, and collected.

Even though this system dates back to the early-mid-2010s, it has just recently acquired global prominence. A jpeg by digital artist Beeple auctioned for $69 million, making it the most costly digital image ever. Ever since, individual developers have created an ever-growing number of digital items and offered them on NFT markets like OpenSea, Rarible, and Nifty Gateway.

Despite the widespread attention, designers feel that the technology's true potential has yet to be discovered. "You may earn a fast buck and maybe get some nice press out of it if you're fortunate, but other possibilities are lurking in the bushes," Christodoulou added. "Now is the right time to try new things and influence the market," he continued. "This is a once-in-a-lifetime chance."

Kerry Murphy, co-owner of virtual fashion firm The Fabricant, believes that decentralization of power will affect other sectors. "You could stay on your sofa all day doing something you enjoy and making a career doing it – that's the possibility that NFTs offers for every single creative business," he told Dezeen. "I'm not saying it'll happen quickly, but once it does, the impact will be huge."

The Possibilities are Limitless

Designers expect that NFTs will flood new artworks utilizing digital tools like augmented and virtual reality. Both Christodolou and Bocci, a Canadian lighting company, are exploring time-based programmable assets, digital visuals that change over time or react to their owners.

The startup, which is already offering DIY candle directions as an NFT, looks into how the system may mirror a product's manufacturing process. "Time-based programmable assets excite me as they may interconnect and assist these procedures," said Bocci owner Omer Arbel to Dezeen. Krista Kim, a US artist that auctioned the "world's first NFT digital apartment" for almost half a million dollars, believes that with the advancement of AR, her digital apartment will become a location where people can socialize.

She told Dezeen, "The possibilities of NFTs as a platform extends much beyond simply displaying images and films on a screen." "It will be turned into 3D programmable assets that can be viewed through AR and manipulated by users."

She went on to say, "The potential is limitless." "We are going to witness a creative and artistic revolution when AR is completely liberated in our real-time and space," said French artist Joanie Lemercier. "Not many possibilities have been tested." "I don't expect the short video clips and image files that are popular right now to be the best we can accomplish."

Designers may "easily interact with the audience" with NFTs. NFTs have enabled 3D artists with large social media fanbases, like Wannerstedt, Reisinger, and Christodoulou, to monetize their artwork. Artists can also incorporate royalties into NFTs so that when their artwork is transferred to a new buyer, they earn a share of the earnings.

As a result, the artists claim they can devote more time to direct customer work. "I work all days in a week for commercial businesses and need to do my job in the mornings and evenings," Christodoulou explained. "I get to set aside a month for R&D and really explore some unique ideas for my next NFT release."

The Surge and Plunge Ethereum and NFTs

After Bitcoin, the second-largest crypto is more than just digital money; it's the bedrock of a billion-dollar industry. Understand the dynamics in action behind the emergence of Ethereum from digital art. A rather funny title emerged in the New York Times business section:

Why did a $600,000 animated flying cat with a Pop-Tart body sell? If you were online in 2011, you are most likely familiar with that cat. Chris Torres, the creator of the web's most popular "nyan cat" GIF (which depicts a pixel-art kitten blasting into space on a rainbow), had sold his several-year-old meme for about $600,000.

Torres wasn't alone in discovering a means to monetize digital art that was formerly regarded essentially worthless, owing to the fact anybody can copy and paste a digital file indefinitely. In the last few weeks, we've seen:

Christie's has announced plans to sell the world's first "fully digital" piece, a series of pictures produced by Beeples that will begin at $100. A $1.5 million sale was made on a nice-looking lo-fi monkey from the Cryptopunks series. $450,000 was raised through a set of 3D models for "crazy furniture," such as a table made of bubble gum.

Mark Cuban, the owner of the Dallas Mavericks, sold just a tweet for $952. Every one of these tales had one thing in common: people paying considerable real cash for a virtual, digital-world item. A class of crypto assets known as NFTs has enabled this budding industry. An NFT (short for "non-fungible token") is a certificate of authenticity that certifies that your copy of an infinitely copy-pasteable digital asset (be it an image, a movie, music, or anything else) is the genuine item.

NFTs are typically transacted on the Ethereum blockchain network, which uses its "smart contract" capability and can be acquired or traded on specific NFT markets. (Even they're just getting a lot of attention now, NFTs aren't exactly new. You may recall the 2017 Cryptokitties fad, a virtual cat trading game.)

An NFT, like Bitcoin, is a token that can be purchased or sold on marketplaces that specialize in such transactions. However, unlike Bitcoin, each coin has almost similar features. Each NFT represents a unique digital asset. (Thus the term "non-fungible.") They've been used for trading everything, including celebrity memorabilia and NBA "digital artifacts" to a digital apartment and live Deadmau5 videos.

NFTs have spurred philosophical arguments about the nature of ownership as they've grown into an unexpectedly significant industry, with projected sales of over $100 million. Is acquiring digital collectibles that different from acquiring unique sneakers, vinyl music, or even Picassos?

Although they don't even begin to scratch the surface of a larger story that NFTs can help us grasp, these are intriguing topics. In the larger picture, smart contract technology drives a novel, decentralized alternative to the present banking system, allowing artists, meme-makers, and music artists to sell their digital items. Capital will move via open-source protocols that are fast, simpler, more open, and accessible to everyone in that alternative system intended to liberate everyone financially.

How NFTs Could Change the World

CryptoKitties—think digital Beanie Babies—launched in 2017 and established the framework for the digital-art craze. Fans have spent over $32 million on these massive-eyed, unique cartoon cats, which they have collected, traded, and bred. In the meantime, video gamers have been splashing the cash on aesthetic improvements for their avatars, with Fortnite players spending an average of $82 on in-game stuff in 2019, greatly mainstreaming the decision to spend real cash on digital assets. At the same time, the worth of cryptos has soared, propelled in part by famous supporters such as Elon Musk and Mark Cuban. Bitcoin, for example, has increased by more than 1,000 percent in the last year, and anything, even crypto-related, even NFTs, has been caught up in a frenzy.

Big corporations and individuals are joining in the thrill: According to parent firm Dapper Labs, NBA Top Shot, the NBA's exclusive network for buying and selling NFT-based highlights (organized as digital trading cards), has accumulated more than $390 million in sales ever since October launch. NFT trade cards featuring Super Bowl highlights were bought for more than $1.6 million by football star Rob Gronkowski, while NFT songs were auctioned for almost $2 million by rock band Kings of Leon. Jack Dorsey, the founder of Twitter, sold his first ever tweet as an NFT, fetching an awesome $2.9 million. The last few years have been a feasting craze, with new highs appearing on a near-daily basis. After his phenomenon auction, Beeple said to fans and partners convened on chat app Clubhouse, "I'm very fucking overwhelmed right now."

Investors that view NFT art merely as an item to be purchased low and sold high, on the other hand, are throwing money into the pockets of artists. For years, Los Angeles-based artist Andrew Benson has experimented with psychedelic, glitchy digital video work. He's gotten work in museums and galleries, but he's also worked at a software firm and done commission work for artists like M.I.A. and Aphex Twin to make ends meet. "I've always believed that the greatest way to live as an artist is not to have to live as an artist," Benson explains.

Benson was tormented with worry about his career in the art industry a year and a half ago when his intentions to present a new series of videos fell through. He recalls wondering to himself, "Do I even want to go through the hassle of attempting to do this sort of work and searching somewhere to present it?" In January, a friend that works at Foundation, an NFT platform, encouraged Benson to enter a piece on the blockchain. Benson didn't really think much about it, although he did send along a clip that he claims might have otherwise "gone on a website or something." The work, which resembles a kinetic, multicolored Rorschach, went for $1,250 in just ten days. Benson has since sold ten more paintings in a similar price range. He's now considering a future whereby he could only depend on his art to support himself. "It rattled my worldview, to be honest," he recalls. "Watching this piece find a meaning and a place where it counts inspires me to feel more like an artist."

NFT collectors also show a strong enthusiasm in many other artists who work in avant-garde and occasionally controversial approaches. Hyper-referential (and often vulgar) cartoons, as well as spinning 3-D renderings, street-style oversaturated color schemes, and hyper-referential (and often vulgar) art, are all prospering. A smaller generation trained on Insta and a rabble-rousing cryptocurrency clientele is drawn to some of these Internet-triggered trends. According to Dryhurst, "the street art and countercultural trends are being exploited to support the image that most finance-cryptocurrency people have that they are the 'punks' in the greater technology and finance world."

Many in the traditional art industry are stunned by these changes. "A lot of traditional collectors explore the NFT world and can't seem to fit it into any suitable system of belief," says Wendy Cromwell, an art adviser in New York. "We're at a critical juncture: many of the most knowledgeable individuals in the art space are getting older and don't have the desire or mental capacity to decipher the Internet's jargon." Following Christie's Beeple sale, competing auction house Sotheby's swiftly declared its collaboration with NFT artist Pak, demonstrating that, though art powerhouses may not grasp the style, they do grasp its lucrative potential.

A novel generation of digital artists is grouping in tight-knit NFT groups, with or without the approval of the mainstream, mirroring previous generations of artists spanning disciplines and genres hanging out and inspiring each other's ideas, techniques, and work. "In the space, there is a big culture of generosity," Benson adds. "In the domains of independent music and fine art, there is usually a feeling that one artist will emerge victorious from a scene. There is a sense of wealth with this, and it appears as everyone may benefit."

Whales and minnows have been seen swimming together in rare circumstances. A collecting group named Metapurse, two unnamed Singapore-based investors, exploring with tech-supported collective-ownership concepts, proved to be the buyer of the $69 million Beeple work. Both bought 20 Beeple art pieces, put them in a virtual museum that anybody can view for free, and then fractionalized their new business into coins that 5,400 individuals currently possess. Their value surged sixfold. The duo is planning a related idea with their recent headline-grabbing buying plan to showcase in a top-notch virtual museum. According to Metapurse co-founder Twobadour, the goal is to "open up both the experience of art and the ownership of art to everyone."

Chapter 7:
CO-INVESTING IN ART AND LUXURY COLLECTIBLES

Co-investing in Art

While co-investing works of art is not a new concept, art collectors are increasingly turning to co-investing schemes to diversify their art portfolios and share the high carrying costs of art ownership.

How Art Co-investment Arrangements Created

In most cases, art co-investments are established through the co-investment agreement (oral or written) or the formation of a jointly owned "special purpose vehicle" (SPV) to acquire one or more artworks.

If an SPV is formed, the parties must first choose a legal entity and then prepare the SPV's governing documents to clarify the nature of the co-investment arrangement. Annual expenses for the ownership, management, storage, and transportation of the artwork are often shared net pay by the SPV's investors, based on their investment interests in the artwork.

Important Mechanism of Co-Investment Relationship Mechanics

Whenever you are drafting a co-investment agreement, you should tackle and agree on the following decisions concerning the subject of artwork:

Ownership Interests

The particular ownership interests of the multiple co-owners in the collectively owned work must be explicitly described, either in the co-ownership contract or in the underpinning equity interests of each party in the SPV that owns the designated artwork.

If the participants are prepared to share profit interests and/or liabilities for covering the costs of owning the work other than based on their basic rate payment of the purchase price, such notions must be stated expressly in the co-ownership contract or the operating documents of the SPV, as applicable.

Storage costs, insurance premiums, transit charges, cataloging costs, legal expenses to safeguard the artwork against rival ownership claims or attribution concerns, preservation costs, and legal fees associated with purchase/sale contracts, consignment contracts, and contracts, in specific, should be agreed upon by the parties.

Additionally, the partners must discuss what will happen if one of them fails to fulfill their ownership obligations. One logical solution is for the non-defaulting side to fund the defaulting party's ownership expenses at a set interest rate. Any revenues from the sale of the co-owned artwork are first deducted from the advance amount and accumulated interest.

Improving Returns on Investments

Purchasing artwork can feel more like a game of chance than a wise investment. As a result of the high-profile auction sales, painting and sculpture collectors have recently created a lot of excitement in the fine art market. This is due to a $91.1 million rabbit sculpture that set a new world record. It was the most expensive work ever sold by a living artist when it was auctioned in May 2019.

Investing in valuable artwork can indeed pay off handsomely. Investing in art, however, comes with its own set of risks and cons.

Investing in Art

Extensive study is required for any financial venture. Spend many months passively observing art auction news and valuation patterns before diving into the snares of the fine art market. Speak with a curator or art specialist to acquire a better idea of high-value art items and artists. They may be able to provide you with insider information.

In general, the works of a prominent living artist are valued at a lower value than those of a deceased master artist whose works are limited in quantity. As a result, art created by deceased writers or painters sells for more and grows in value faster than art created by living artists.

Don't be intimidated by collectors and advisors until you've gained enough expertise to enter the market and attend an art sale. Gallery curators frequently go to considerable pains to teach their extensive knowledge of art history to collectors. The advice and information provided by gallery specialists can sometimes dispute your inner impression regarding the work's value. As a result, internet art auctions provide a less frightening setting for first-time art buyers.

To summarize, art investing is a difficult task. A buyer must assess the artist's total effect beyond media appreciation and press attention for artwork to create large profits.

Does Art Investing Pay Off?

Buying art is an example of a nontraditional investment technique. It can be a hugely successful venture for astute art buyers.

Tips for Investing in Art as a Beginner

- Be cautious of the risks

Art is a speculative asset type with limited liquidity. If you're seeking to make quick cash by flipping an undervalued piece of art, think again. Your art item may take years to sell at auction. As a result, it's always a good idea to think about art investing as a medium- to long-term investment.

Diversify your collection by collecting art from various artists, artistic traditions, and historical periods to reduce the risks associated with art acquisition.

- Be a part of the community

Start creating a professional network in the fine art field and attend art fairs and auctions regularly to increase your chances of making a smart art purchase.

The Right Time to Sell

Investing in art is unlike most other types of investments. Technically, it's better to think of it as an asset that grows in value over time – an asset you choose based on your own personal preferences and enjoyment.

There is no up-to-date answer, but there are a few key considerations to keep in mind when deciding when and how to sell your art. It's a safe bet that you'll be able to sell a piece of artwork you just bought in about ten years, maybe five if you bought at the right time.

- **Appreciation**

While this "slow and steady wins the race" method isn't particularly glamorous, it's very good news for art investors.

The art market has been increasing in value for the last 50 years or so, and the trend has been fairly consistent. Purchasing artwork from a collectible artist allows you to participate in this steadily growing market. If you wait until the right time to sell, a quality piece of artwork by a successful artist could increase in value by 20-30 percent.

- **Don't sell your house too soon.**

If the value of your artwork appears to have increased, you may want to sell it as soon as possible. However, even if the artwork's value has increased, selling too soon is unlikely to yield a significant profit.

Certain fees, such as finder's or buyer's fees, artist's resale rights, and others, are associated with reselling. If you're trying to sell a piece of artwork that has only increased in value by 10%, you might not be able to recoup your initial investment

- **Think About the Buyer**

Keep in mind that you are not the only one who has observed an increase in an artist's output. Everyone else in your position are going to be expecting an ideal moment to market their art. For artists, these are excellent opportunities, as a recent spike in popularity might imply new fans, followers, and collectors interested in investing in the artist. If too many established owners attempt to sell their artwork at the same time, the market will become saturated, diluting what ought to have been higher demand.

- **Inquire About It**

If you're not sure about the proper moment to sell, getting other people's comments or recommendations can help. Seeking an expert dealer for a detailed view of the market is indeed a wonderful approach to gain an insight knowledge of the industry, particularly if you plan to sell soon. You may also inquire about other collectors who buy and sell the works of other creatives. They may not be familiar with the piece you're seeking to sell, but the more art market knowledge they have, the more advise they'll be able to provide.

Co-investing in Collectibles

Your basement and garage may be stuffed with old furniture, books, and other items you've kept over the years if you have a lot of storage space. It may appear to be nothing more than a pile of trash at first look. However, if you sift through your belongings attentively, there's a probability you're sitting on a few precious collectibles that are just waiting to make you money.

Collectibles are worth significantly more than their initial cost. They are categorized as asset classes that do not fit into any other categories, such as stocks, bonds, cash, or real estate. Investing in this asset class can be both lucrative and beneficial to your financial goals. However, knowing the fundamentals is beneficial. This book examines collectibles as an investment and will assist you in determining whether or not such a sensitive market is a good place to put your investment.

All Things Old Made New Again

Anything that can be sold for more money than it was initially worth is considered a collectible. These are products that appreciate with time. Some goods are mass-produced to become collectibles. Pictures and numerous works of art, for example, are collectibles that spark the interest of collectors. To get the most profit out of a collectible, the owner must make sure it is in great condition. Some of the most well-known collectibles include trading cards, postcards, and comic strips. Here are a couple of examples:

140,000,000 B.C. is the date of the beginning of time. A baby Allosaurus dinosaur became entangled in a sinkhole tucked away in the undergrowth. An amateur paleontologist helped him out—or at least what was left of his head—millions of years later. The repaired skull of the Allosaurus sold for $600 in 2005.

The year 1908. Honus Wagner of the Pittsburgh Pirates hit his tenth home run of the season and finished the year with a.354 batting average, one of the best years in his career. The American Tobacco Company honored Wagner the following year by including a playing card in its cigarette packets. Only around 60 made it into stores before the world learned that Honus was a staunch anti-smoker. Wagner's cigarette trade card went for $1.1 million on eBay in 2000.

In the year 1962, In addition to rescuing the world, Stan Lee developed a character concerned about paying his rent, caring for his ill aunt, and passing his next school test. The cover price of Peter Parker's misadventure with a radioactive spider was $0.12.The first edition of The Amazing Spider-Man was among the most valuable comics in 2006, with a price of $6,000 or more.

Reasons to Buy Collectibles

There are a lot of reasons why you shouldn't buy collectibles. You won't always get a high return on your item, and there's no guarantee that anyone else will be interested in what you're selling. The only reason to purchase them maybe for your own benefit. That isn't to say you should avoid them entirely.

People don't buy collectibles to invest in them; they buy them to spend money on. If you are lucky, you will be able to sell that same product in the future for more money than you paid for it during the time you bought it.

Tips on Buying and Selling Collectibles

Heirlooms Should Be Preserved

If you've inherited antiques or artifacts from your kins, do some research to determine if they're worth anything before tossing them into a dank attic corner. The return on investment on a collection increases when you pay nothing for it.

Call and Compare

Take a minute to think and phone other sellers and price out similar things if you have your eye on a collectible. Yes, there will always be "two interested purchasers" the very next day, but you should not make hasty selections if the dealer is pressuring you. The best approach is to look around the store and then phone the dealer when you arrive home. In the long run, you'll think more clearly and have less remorse. Purchase from other collectors if at all possible. Because they'll presume you have the same pricing range as they do, they'll be less inclined to inflate things.

Ask for a Written Guarantee

Ask the seller to write a buy-back guarantee for an agreed period if a collection is truly an "unfathomable buy" with "many interested purchasers." After all, the dealer can repurchase it at the same price and resell it to all those eager purchasers pounding on the doors.

Insurance for Collectibles is a factor to consider

Considering the hazards that come with owning precious objects, collectibles insurance may be a good investment. These insurance safeguard your collectibles from unforeseen events such as unintentional breakage, vandalism, flooding, and other sorts of losses. While collectors of precious objects may require this level of security, your collection does not need to be worth millions to be worth insuring.

Final Thoughts

There are other ways to protect against inflation. A collectible is a taxable, illiquid investment that generates no income and may lose value if dropped. If you're going to buy one, make sure it's one you'll be able to enjoy for the rest of your life rather than relying on a possible future sale.

Chapter 8:
SUCCESS & FAILURES

NFTs Help Artists Solve Vital Problem

Kevin Abosch, a New York-based artist, has sold a $1.5 million painting of a potato, created a neon artwork inspired by cryptocurrencies, and even auctioned his blood on the blockchain network.

In several respects, the 51-year-old Irish artist's entry into the non-fungible tokens (NFTs) space was the natural next step for his work, which investigates digital currency and value themes. Non-fungible tokens (NFTs) are digital tokens that prove a digital collectible's authenticity and ownership. The technology has been present since at least 2017 and is a spinoff of the cryptocurrency industry that uses the blockchain.

Is it possible for anyone to become an NFT collector?

However, in March, the NFT frenzy reached new heights when Christie's, the famed art auction house, sold off a digital collage by an artist known as Beeple for about $70 million, instantly making him the of the most expensive living artist ever.

Many people are perplexed as to why someone would like to acquire an NFT. For artists like Abosch, NFTs assist in resolving a long-standing dilemma in digital art: how can you take possession of something that can be readily and continuously reproduced? What does it imply to own art in the first place?

Abosch began working on a series of images in 2020 that dealt with encryption and alphanumeric codes. Following the cancellation of many of his in-person presentations due to the Covid-19 outbreak, Abosch felt that now was the ideal time to sell his work as NFTs. He planned to sell them on OpenSea, the world's leading token market, that receives 1.5 million weekly visits and triggered $95 million in sales in February 2021 alone.

He made a $2 million gain from the collection, including all work that can't be physically moved to a gallery or put on display. He became the most popular NFT artist on the OpenSea marketplace as a result of it. On the eve of the auction in March 2021, he told the Guardian that the notion that art should be a tangible product that can be exhibited is soon becoming obsolete.

"Some individuals are troubled by this concept since they wish to know what you genuinely own," he explained. "However, persons of a younger generation do not have this problem.

"Wanting to grasp something in your hand is a very outdated tradition as if the ethereal or immaterial has no value."

An NFT auction functions similarly to an online auction on sites like eBay. Every work is shown as an image file with metadata – that simply means "data about data" – including the title, number, and who owns it.

Abosch's 1111 series debuted on OpenSea at 11:11 a.m. EST, where he posted 111 works for a limited time. Following the beginning of the auction, prospective purchasers visit the Abosch sale page to bid on specific works of art - in this case, using the crypto Ethereum.

While the NFTs were traded on Opensea, the real sequence of characters that links the owner to their new NFT is saved on Arweave, a program that acts as a form of permanent internet by storing files in perpetuity over a decentralized network of systems, preventing them from being erased or damaged in the future.

To put it another way, a buyer will pay for an image on the NFT trading site OpenSea with an Ethereum token and receive an Arweave address certifying the acquisition and ownership of the image file in exchange. In the end, 53 different collectors bought 106 of the 111 works, with the most costly selling for $21,242.

Some artists, including Abosch, are attracted to the NFT tech because of its democratizing nature: anybody can connect and buy the items, and the work comes with a publicly available ledger of its full history - when it was minted, who possessed it, who bought it, and for how much. This, according to Abosch, is a break from previous art purchases, wherein investors put precious art in-store to hold it for a period when it will be more expensive.

The prominence of cryptocurrencies and the increase of art market speculation have been growing rapidly for some time. However, the coronavirus outbreak has further positioned the sector for the triumph of tech like NFTs, according to Andrei Pesic, an art history professor at Stanford.

"As we've had to transfer so much of our life online in the years 2020 and 2021, it has actually opened or hastened the idea of pricing digital products in the same manner that we value physical products," he said. Abosch, who has been utilizing blockchain technology to mint art since 2013, says the NFT mania was sparked by two factors: the tech is really intriguing and practical, and any new bright thing that promises to make people rich quickly will readily attract attention.

"We are in a significant evolutionary time – it's like we're in the middle of the biggest storm, except instead of everything being damaged, we'll see new constructions that are quite fascinating," he explained. "However, there will be some rubble."

The Old Art World's Problem

- **The Power of Gatekeepers**

The Problem in the Old Art World:

In a fundamentally hierarchical structure, individuals and organizations with lengthy histories, huge money, and pre-existing business connections exert significant power over who gets to participate.

The NFT Difference:

New, decentralized markets can accept artists and participants without the sanction of the art establishment. While some NFT marketplaces (like SuperRare and Nifty Gateway) will only welcome artists by invite or registration, for the time being, others (such as Rarible) will enable any enthusiastic artist to begin trading in their market.

Ameer Suhayb Carter, an expert cryptocurrency designer and advisor preparing to launch the Well Protocol, an NFT network, archive, and support system with a particular emphasis on BIPOC and LGBTQIA artists, exemplifies the blockchain art world's most transformative power.

"In many situations, these are folks that can't even find a job in their home country. Carter, who also operates as an artist under the nickname Sirsu, told Artnet News, "We're giving voice to the voiceless."

"The idea is for them to be able to establish the communities they want in their way. I provide them the tools they need to take control of their lives. I'm not going to build for you; I'm going to build with you."

- **The Collectors' Values**

The Problem in the Old Art World:

The changing structure of upper-echelon art acquisition is part of what makes existing gatekeepers so strong. Investors fight to represent the same types of artists that buyers crave: artists who look like them, that is, persons who are primarily white and male who have contacts within the high-art society.

The NFT Difference:

Until now, many, if not all, NFT purchasers have come from outside the conventional art business circles, and they have shown minimal concern in recognized investors', advisers', and collectors' ideas on what is worth collecting—and at what price.

According to Kevin McCoy, the artist who built the first NFT as part of Rhizome's Seven on Seven conference in 2014, "the cash flowing into the NFTs space is cash that was already in the space." "Cryptocurrency investors are buying NFTs. I've constantly believed that fresh makers and collectors, not the old art world, are the source of power."

- **Wealth Redistribution**

The Problem in the Old Art World:

When it comes to profiting from art, practically all of the significant benefits go to the collector on resale. Even the most successful artists are usually only paid a pittance in resale royalties. The UK, for instance, has a resale royalty maximum of €12,500 (about $17,300) for its inhabitants, regardless of how much a work sells for when it is resold; the US, on the other hand, has no resale royalty at all—at least, not outside of revenue generated in California during a one-year time in the late 1970s.

The NFT Difference:

Since percentage-based resale royalties may be built into the conditions of each NFT sale, creatives can profit appropriately and indefinitely as their pieces travel through the market.

Most importantly, this redistributive mechanism can be completely automated. What is the reason for this? Because the "smart contract," a collection of instructions that operates on the blockchain network without human involvement if independently verifiable conditions are satisfied, is the basic mechanism of NFT exchanges. (For example, "ownership of this asset goes to the sender as soon as the sales price enters the present owner's account," state hypothetically.)

According to Amy Whitaker, a professor of visual arts administration at New York University that began exploring blockchain in 2014, the potential get much more exciting when NFT artists utilize smart contracts to redistribute assets to more than just themselves.

For any prospective NFT pieces, artist Sara Ludy reportedly arranged a new sales share with her New York gallery, bitforms: 50% for Ludy, 15% for the NFT network, and 35% for bitforms—with the latter amount equally distributed in 7% increments between the gallery's founder and four employees.

Whitaker compared the move to a tip jar for restaurant employees. It's a way of "collectivizing economics," as well as "trying to combine for-profit and nonprofit frameworks so individuals can route some of the earnings towards grantmaking or charity" without having to fill out extra tax forms if the creators so desire.

- **Preservation and Ownership**

The Problem in the Old Art World:

Possession of (and copyright of) works like installation, performance, and video sometimes devolves into a quagmire of misunderstanding outside traditional physical media.

Investors and creators must create term sheets from the start for every piece, with the final papers typically veering between unnecessarily plain and frustratingly complicated. All for the collector to regularly misinterpret or ignore their responsibilities, particularly when it comes to the long-term care of the piece.

The NFT Difference:

The blockchain network stores the work's full provenance and copyright information and the possibility to add a wealth of additional data that would be useful to historians and archivists. Standard contracts, such as ERC-721, are widely used by artists unsure about establishing their own agreements. Should a disagreement over intellectual property emerge, an NFT's whole transaction history may be audited back to its creation, providing irrefutable "on-chain" evidence of which party's rights are valid.

Possible Environmental Implication of NFT

On March 8, 2021, the online market ArtStation made a contentious declaration for which it was obliged to apologize within hours publicly. The corporation published a statement saying, "We are very sorry for all the unpleasant emotions this has generated." "We definitely made a mistake and accepted responsibility. It was entirely our fault."

The apology was issued in reaction to online criticism of ArtStation's plans to build a new platform for non-fungible tokens (NFTs). This multi-billion-dollar fad has sparked outrage from environmentalists since it first gained popular attention in 2021. While a few in the art world believe NFTs is a passing craze with no underlying real-world value — the digital pieces sold could still be duplicated and distributed for free by anybody online — climate activists warn that their environmental effect is quite real.

"We believe that NFTs is a transformational technology that can bring major, positive change for digital artists," ArtStation said in a statement, announcing the cancellation of the new project. "We hope to develop a solution that is both egalitarian and environmentally good at some point in the future."

The underpinning blockchain network that allows NFTs, a type of online ledger that also permits cryptos like bitcoin, has sparked criticism. Cryptos and NFTs, to function, need a system of electricity-consuming devices to run their blockchain technology. The environmental effect of Bitcoin has been well recorded, with a University of Cambridge study claiming that its technology currently uses more power than the entire Netherlands.

The study on the electricity needs of NFTs is less well-developed, and it has sparked debate among individuals in the crypto sector. CryptoArt.wtf, a site that tracked the environmental effect of NFT marketplaces, was shut down, with the website's proprietors alleging it was used "as a vehicle for discrimination and bullying." Memo Akten, the site's owner and a digital artist, concluded that the average NFT has an environmental impact equal to that of somebody residing in the EU every month.

According to some estimations, "selling a 100-piece version has a carbon footprint of almost 10 tonnes CO2, far above the EU's per capita annual impact — including all emissions from industry and commerce." Beeple, whose work Everydays: The First 5000 Days sold for $69 million at Christies, is one of the most well-known creators who benefited from NFTs.

Beeple has vowed to put his profits in renewable energy and carbon capture initiatives to make his art pieces carbon neutral or negative. Besides just mitigating the emissions, there are various approaches to make NFTs more environmentally conscious. To begin with, blockchains might be fueled by renewable energy sources, which is currently happening in China due to a ban on coal-burning server farms and the advent of environmentally friendly alternatives.

The second and more practical option is to change the blockchain's protocol from Proof-of-Work (PoW) to Proof-of-Stake (PoS) (PoS), something we will discuss extensively later in this book. This method, which ethereum, the world's second most valued crypto, is considering, consumes no energy because the ledger is protected by users "staking" their crypto tokens.

In a previous 'Guide to ecofriendly CryptoArt (NFTs),' a group of creators led by Memo Akten noted, "There are more responsible paths emerging." "Hopefully, as more creators flock to these new seas, networks, developers, dealers, and collectors will collaborate to create more environmentally sustainable and transparent systems."

Artists Issues from Minting Arts and Collectibles on the Blockchain

Potential Claims by Holders of Rights in Underlying Works

Creators have recently stated on social media that their paintings have been "created" into NFTs and sold without their consent. OpenSea's Terms of Service, for instance, enable copyright holders to lodge complaints and state that the site "will remove works in respect to official copyright accusations and will cancel a participant's access to the Services if the user is proved to be a serial infringer."

Rightsholders, on the other hand, may pursue legal action. The artist or other rights holders may choose to file a copyright violation lawsuit against the sellers or makers of the NFTs.

Who gets to prosecute is determined by who owns the rights: the artist or the actual artwork's owner. Except if the artist has given somebody else a right in a written agreement, the artist is the only person who can prosecute for violation of the right to create derivative pieces, like digital images.

The possession of copyright could become considerably more complicated. Artists that developed the work under an employment agreement with somebody and subsequently attempted to make digital creations based on the original piece using NFTs could face legal action. The original piece may be a work for hire, as defined by 17 U.S.C. 101, were in the ownership, and the license to base derivative pieces on it belongs to the employer (or commissioning party), not the creator. In the production of comic characters and related art, movie movies, and certain musical recordings, this is frequently the case. For instance, in a letter published in multiple media sources last week, DC Comics urged its freelancers not to sell NFTs of works centered on DC Comics characters. The copyright owner may have allegations for breach of contract following the artist's original agreement or freelance contract. Questions of copyright infringement are expected to arise.

There will also be disagreements over whether the NFT is fair usage. Suppose the NFT incorporates an innovative work of expression, versions a full physical artwork, and can deny the copyright holder of income from the use of the work. In that case, some of the questions will need to be determined. However, this has not been put to the test. While no such matter relating the selling of NFTs in the United States seems to have been determined yet, rights owners may claim that such exploitation of their creation is a copyright infringement under current law. In such circumstances, the fair use criterion outlined in Blanch v. Koons, 467 F.3d 244, would be applied (2d Cir. 2006).

Potential Claims by Buyers of NFTs

Since NFTs are such a new form of commerce, some NFT owners would likely claim that they misinterpreted the scope of their rights when they bought one. A contract or the terms of service of a market platform may define the extent of what is obtained. However, those terms may mention (or fail to disclose) that others could still be able to access, view, or listen to the NFT-minted work. They may also mention (or omit to indicate) that the buyer will not benefit from the usage of the underlying video clip or image file. The buyer of many NFTs does not obtain the rights to the said work. Except if the entities formally consented to impart copyright ownership, buyers will not have a rights interest in the artworks, and creators do not forfeit copyright protection over pieces when bought, according to SuperRare. Based on the situation, the provisions may also allow for the sale of additional copies or versions of the same NFT. If the buyer feels the extent of what he or she was buying was not completely revealed or misunderstood, and the worth has declined, the buyer may file a fraud charge or seek to rescind the contract. A buyer who feels a seller of an NFT has broken the contract terms may file a case against the seller or artist of the NFT based on the particular contract. If extra versions of a piece were issued despite the contract specifying that the piece is a special edition NFT, the buyer could file a case for breach of contract.

Buyers of NFTs that allege they were deceived about buying from the artist or legitimate works by a certain artist may initiate fraud or breach of contract charges against the dealer. Though blockchain verification should lessen the ownership risks connected with purchasing a specific NFT, it will not eradicate the traditional authenticity difficulties involved with tangible pieces of art. Skilled fraudsters have been able to duplicate the look of the actual artists' pieces of intangible works, and digital artists will seek to do the same with NFTs. For instance, an NFT may use an image file by a certain artist and be sold as such, even though the creator had no involvement in its production and did not allow the usage of images. Before purchasing an NFT, buyers are expected to do the same level of credibility and provenance due diligence as before buying a tangible piece of art.

Buyers may be apprehensive about market speculation considering the fast-paced market and high prices for previous NFT transactions. "Wash trading" is a type of market manipulation employed in fungible token marketplaces, primarily to inflate a crypto exchange's reported trading activity, rendering it more appealing to prospective traders and customers. NFT marketplaces, like other markets, may be subject to manipulation methods that create false demand, leading to possible fraud and other allegations.

Buyers seeking to enter the NFT marketplace must first acquaint themselves with the conditions of what they are purchasing and the extent of what will be delivered to safeguard themselves. They must also conduct as much due diligence on the seller and the platform as feasible. This involves looking over the Terms of Service, which often include arbitration clauses.

NFTs and Regulatory Problems

NFTs also pose regulatory problems, which are beyond the scope of this chapter. NFTs could be liable to safety and trade restrictions, anti-money laundering and corruption laws, and other prohibitions, which sellers and purchasers ought to be aware of. Because the buyer or seller of an NFT can be wherever on the earth, players in the NFT marketplace must assess if they conform with US law and international and regional regulations. Determine if blocked individuals are trying to flee sanctions by using NFTs. The Office of Foreign Asset Control (OFAC) released a statement in October 2020, emphasizing that high-value art trades "could play a significant role in blocked persons entering the U.S. market and financial system in violation of OFAC regulations," and indicating that OFAC does not accept the art exclusion in the "Berman Amendment" to the International Emergency Economic Powers Act (IEEPA) and the Traditional Exchange Control Act

Financial statement requirements should be considered by all entities involved in a transaction. The Financial Crimes Enforcement Network (FinCEN) proposed regulations to explain documentation and reporting obligations for financial firms regarding cryptocurrencies that would reduce the reporting requirement for transactions that start or end outside the United States from $3,000 to $250. On March 9, 2021, FinCEN issued a notice urging financial institutions to disclose inappropriate activity involving the trading in antiquities and art.

Chapter 9:
HOW TO BE A CRYPTO ARTIST

How to create your own NFTs

It's astonishing how straightforward and easy it is to create your NFTs. The most common marketplace for minting NFTs are OpenSea and Rarible. But even though Rarible is more successful in overall sales, OpenSea provides premium features, such as the ability to use the OpenSea exchange to create your NFT webstore. Participants can put their piece of art on the webstore and create catalogs on the platforms without having any prior knowledge of blockchain network.

Nevertheless, you should be aware that there will be certain initial costs. A blockchain network, usually Ethereum's, governs NFTs. So, to tokenize your art piece or item, you'll be charged a network fee that is referred to as gas fee.

Rarible allows creatives to mint their NFTs on the blockchain during the creation process (on-chain). This results in lower prices on a regular basis. Rarible is usually the right option if you intend to make a huge amount of money from a few NFTs

. Nevertheless, you could use OpenSea's Collection Manager to create numerous and cheaper NFTs.

OpenSea participants will mint a new NFTs set for a one-time fee. From such a set, the OpenSea highly centralized unit could generate an endless number of NFTs and hold them off-chain before selling them. At this point, the buyer will pay the transfer's gas fee, and the NFT would be added to the blockchain and transferred.

We will guide you through the process to create your NFTs in an OpenSea platform.

Step 1: Set up MetaMask

In order to mint your NFT, you'll need to first create a digital wallet. This is where you store your NFTs. In the future, it will equally be used to pay for blockchain network transaction gas fees.

Go to metamask.io to download the software or add the chrome extension. It's easy and free to build a MetaMask wallet. Keep records of your seed phrase should you need to retrieve the wallet in the future.

Wallets are not used to store crypto or NFTs. Instead, they are used to store your private key, which is necessary to authorise blockchain transactions. The blockchain technology stores both cryptos and NFTs, whereas the wallet ID is needed to determine who owns them.

Step 2: Tokenize your Art

You can mint your NFTs when you've created a wallet. On opensea.io, select the Create option from the list menu. You may then connect your wallet to OpenSea and get to business.

Select the Add New Item tab after giving your NFT series a label. You can now upload the file you would like to tokenize and customize it with features and statistics to set it apart from the rest of your collection.

Decide how many copies of every item you'll need, then set a retail price.

Step 3: List on the marketplace

Before you can market your first NFT, you ought to grant OpenSea access to sell items from your account. Because this is a blockchain technology trade, you'll have to pay a transaction gas fee. You're set to make transaction once you transfer Ethereum to your MetaMask account. This fee is only required the first time you mint an NFT collection.

If you don't already have Ether, you can buy it on Coinbase or Gemini and transfer it to your MetaMask account. Anybody can locate and buy your NFTs on the OpenSea market now that you've granted OpenSea permission to sell them. You've completed the task!

The Software Required to Make Digital Art

It can be challenging to pick the best digital art software. There is a plethora of high-quality software available at various price points. We combed through all of the top choices and selected the finest of the lot so you can discover exactly what you're searching for.

You'll like to keep two things in mind: what kind of features you need and how much you are willing to pay for the software. Certain digital art software contains all you need to work with images, from painting to complex image editing. In contrast, others have a more limited collection of capabilities, so you'll have to determine either you want general-purpose or specialized software.

Some of our recommendations are entirely free in cost, while some require a one-time payment and others demand a continuing subscription. You can to discover the right digital art program whether you use a Mac, Windows, iPad, or Linux.

Photoshop

For a long time, Photoshop has been the undisputed leader of the digital art software, but competitors' services are challenging its dominance. Photoshop, on the other hand, remains a tremendously effective and efficient software for digital artists.

Affinity Photo

Affinity Photo doesn't quite match Photoshop's in terms of functionality, particularly with regards to content-aware fill. However, once you gain a sense of it, you'll find it capable of handling many digital art projects.

Corel Painter

The latest edition of Corel Painter has a slew of new features and functions, especially for Apple users. Painter is effective for various styles and processes for photo art, fine art, manga, and concept art. There are over 900 brushes to choose from, as well as numerous customizable options.

Rebelle 4

Features include a massive boost in brush presets to more than 170. Rebelle 4 is described as "one of a kind" paint software that simulates how the paint reacts in the real world. On rebelle 4, your favorite brushes can even be shared and downloaded.

Clip Studio Paint Pro

Clip Studio Paint is gradually becoming the standard software for creating manga and comics. This is the software for you if you want a natural and classic feel bundled up in digital art and painting software. For smooth, realistic-looking pen strokes, Clip Studio Paint employs superior pen pressure detection.

Here is a list of a few other software you may as well consider for your digital artworks

- Artweaver 7
- ArtRage 6
- Krita
- TwistedBrush Pro Studio
- MediBang Paint Pro
- Black Ink
- Paintstorm Studio

Traditional digital art software (adobe)

Now, let's delve a little deep into the most popular digital art software.

Adobe Photoshop is the most well-known and commonly used digital art software. It has a lot of features, is updated frequently, and can be used to make anything from concept thumbnails to comic book pages and even photo-bashed pieces. Photoshop began as a photo-editing software for photographers. It gradually became a standard for many other industries, including digital art.

You may use a wide range of painting tools, brushes, filters, plugins, and layer styles using this software. Because it works efficiently, it has become a well-used industry software for all digital artists in the entertainment sector. Photoshop skills are essential if you want to work in video games, animation, feature films, or any other production company. The learning curve is quite steep. If you're a newbie, all of the functionalities can be overwhelming, and you might get lost in the technical areas of the software. However, once you've mastered the fundamentals, the sky's the limit!

You may create anything in any fashion you like, and you can even modify pictures!

Because Photoshop is the most popular digital art program, there are many Photoshop learning tutorials available online for your use. However, we have provided a short beginner guide below to help you begin your journey with adobe

- Open images: Open images, and create new images

To open and create images

In the menu bar, choose File > Open

To start from scratch and create a new image, Choose File > New from the menu bar. Select a document preset from the drop-down menu. You can change the preset's width and height by entering in your values.

- Get acquainted with your working environment, the user interface

The menu bar (at the very top) displays the File, Edit, Image, and other menus for access to a range of commands, modifications, and panels.

The options bar (below the menu bar) shows you the settings for the tool you're currently using.

Tools for editing images and producing artwork are found in the Tools panel (on the left). Tools that are related are categorized together. You'll be able to discover related features in a group by selecting and holding a tool in the panel.

Color, Layers, Properties, and other panels (on the right) include a wide range of settings for working with images. The complete list of panels can be found under the Window menu.

The document window (in the middle) shows the file you're presently working on. The Document window displays many open documents in tabs.

- Master how to zoom and pan: change your view of an image.

In the Tools panel, you'll find the Zoom tool. In the settings bar, toggle between Zoom In and Zoom Out. You may pan around a large or zoomed-in image with the Hand tool, which is also included in the Tools panel.

- Reverse a command

Undo single or multiple steps, and use the History panel.

To reverse any operation you have executed previously, go to Edit > Undo or click Control+Z (Windows) or Command+Z (macOS).

To repeat any operation you have executed previously, go to Edit > Redo or click Control+Z (Windows) or Command+Z (macOS).

Select Edit > Step Backward numerous times or select a step in the History panel to undo numerous steps.

- Save your work

Make use of the Save command.

Digitizing Tradition or Unorthodox Art into NFTs

Damien Hirst, the richest contemporary artist in the UK, has started to sell his work on the NFT market. Hirst declares that his work with NFTs and crypto sales has been by far the fascinating project he had ever worked on." In a latest run of sales, Hirst was able to make $22.4 million through the auction of 7,481 of his prints to 4,000 people across 67 countries. This figure is perplexing because of the total profit and the enormous volume of prints sold in so many different countries. The usage of cryptocurrency makes it possible to contact 4,000 buyers in 67 countries. As more traditional artists venture into NFTs, accepting this trend will only accelerate, allowing previously unindoctrinated art world participants more accessible.

Christie's New York's Noah Davis, Specialist, Post-War and Contemporary Art, stated that "NFTs have a huge potential in the art market. As a mechanism, the potential for NFTs to change the way we acquire ownership is limitless. The sale's results revealed a lot of excitement in the digital art world and the limitless possibilities of this artistic medium to a larger scope. Digital art is a long-established artistic medium that dates back to the 1950s when individuals were first given access to computer systems. Before the arrival of NFTs and Blockchain technology, assigning value to works created only through digital methods was difficult. All of this is to imply that digital art isn't new; it's only new to the art world, and we see it catch up. We are ecstatic to now have the privilege to use our network to introduce the most forward-thinking artists in this medium to the world art market."

So, would the NFT artworks be judged by the usual academic art world, or will they exist in their parallel ecosystem?" Wendy Cromwell, the creator of boutique consultant Cromwell Art, is positive in this aspect. "The art market follows the money, and ultimately, so do artists," she observes. In the future, she believes the traditional art market will sustain NFTs because, as the quality of NFT art increases, collectors will want to partake.

Copyright your NFTs

The person who buys the NFT has unquestionably acquired the ability to buy and sell that particular NFT. That's all they're going to get. An ownership interest in an NFT does not grant any intellectual property rights. Instead, it gives interest in the acquired digital file. It doesn't matter what the digital file is. Its value is derived from the scarcity of the file rather than the image. An NFT does not guarantee that the person who created it had the legal right to do so in the first place. Many platforms are working to address this issue.

Suppose a user uploads copyrighted work; SuperRare's TOS includes both a DMCA and a refund policy. If somebody paid half a million dollars for a work of art that ended up being illegal and the seller cashed out their cryptocurrency, fled the country, and squandered all of the money, the buyer would be on the hook. Some argue that the remedy is more cryptocurrency and blockchain ledgers, which would allow fraudsters' activities to be traced back, but the world isn't quite there yet.

To put it another way, purchasing an NFT work of digital art is similar to buying a physical work of art. The underlying property right is still owned by the original creatives or artist. If I go to a studio and purchase a painting that I admire, I can't then sell that image to Coca-Cola for use on their cans. That would be a copyright violation. Copyright violation would also occur if I took a photograph of the artwork and sold an NFT replica. If I acquired an NFT copy of it from somebody who didn't have the right to make the NFT in the first place, they (and maybe I) have committed a basic copyright violation with a technological twist.

There is considerable misleading marketing surrounding NFT ownership, leading one to believe that the interest is much broader. Buyer beware!

Build your Brand as an Artist

- Define Who You Are

Attempt to define who you are as an artist? What are you attempting to convey with your artwork? What is the significance of your work to you? What distinguishes your work? Respond to these crucial questions to learn more about yourself as an artist. Consider what your art brand truly entails and how your work differs from that of others. This makes it easier for people to connect with you and your work on a more personal level. It helps people remember you and renders your art more accessible. When you speak of acrylic paints, the Liquitex brand is at the cutting edge of technology. They've developed the world's first cadmium-free colors, giving artists a safer option in their work without sacrificing color power or brightness. Their brand branding is simple, memorable, and has a message to convey. Take note, artists! Potential customers and buyers are more willing to invest in your business if they can connect with you and your art.

- What Do You Aim to Achieve?

As an artist, what do you aim to achieve with your brand? Do you basically wish to share your art with the public and gain more recognition as an artist? Or are you interested in selling your paintings on a part-time basis? Do you want to make a living from your passion for art? You must first identify what you want to achieve to make sure that you are taking the appropriate actions toward reaching your objectives. In financial terms, determine your return on investment, and then build a strategic plan to make that target a reality!

- Spread the Word

Why not check if there are any opportunities to work on art projects or assist one another in reaching out to a larger audience? Alternatively, see if any experienced artists in your neighborhood are ready to offer advice based on their experiences. You could be the one to put your network's artists together. Why not try to build connections with the makers of your preferred creative items, in addition to interacting with other artists? If you genuinely want to increase the visibility of your art, what better way to do so than to collaborate with people who make it possible? Art supply companies frequently collaborate with artists to develop new items. Keeping up with your cherished art supplies company's items and social media networks is a terrific way to start building a relationship.

- Be Accessible

Whether you prefer face-to-face or online activities with your audiences, you must make yourself accessible. Whether you have a physical or virtual store, you must ensure that visitors can simply discover you. Enjoy the benefits of powerful online platforms such as social media to begin. Most individuals today use social media to stay engaged amid the hustle and bustle. Open an account and/or a page on the channels where your fans spend most of their time if you haven't already. Start sharing your art with your friends and family; develop a Facebook "business page" for your artistic brand to provide further information on where people can discover your art - whether you have a physical storefront, sell your art through your website, or use other online resources such as Etsy. Share regular updates on your most recent creative efforts, as well as any artwork that you have for sale. Create Pinterest boards for the many art subjects and platforms you utilize. Keep your Instagram account up to date with stunning photographs and videos of your work.

- Make them want to come back for more

Now that we've covered the essentials, you need to establish brand loyalty to retain your fans and buyers. And, like it or not, brand loyalty isn't just about attempting to sell or share your art with your audience. You, too, would like to reveal a little bit of you. As stated earlier, you want people to relate to you as an artist and your brand. A straightforward method to do this is to use social media to keep in touch with your customers on a more personal level. Share what motivates you to produce art, as well as any important art designs and updates, as well as any advice you can give to other artists.

Building Social Media Following

- Select the appropriate platform

If you work in the digital world, you must have a social media presence. Your social media platforms can serve as a part portfolio, part marketing tool, and part relationships fostering space when adequately managed. Maintaining an up-to-date Twitter or Facebook page is enough to establish credibility and gain the loyalty of your audience and potential customers.

- Create a mailing list.

Although social media networks are beneficial, we must not take them lightly. We'll always be at the mercy of Youtube,

Instagram, or Twitter. They decide whether or not our audience sees our work.

- Create your bio

When a potential follower or buyer stumbles on your social profiles, your bio is the first option they have to learn more about who you are and what you do. Don't leave it empty because it's a chance to stand out and get people's attention.

- Develop a unique creative niche.

It's hard these days to establish a following from the beginning around basic lifestyle content— the net is crowded with creators, so you have to be unique and specific. Identifying the confluence of a demographic and interest or product, such as posters for socially concerned persons, ethical clothes for the androgynous type, or bedding for eco-friendly consumers, is one simple method to do this. Ensure you're creating content (and things) for someone, not just anyone, in anything you do.

- Make a content strategy.

The simplest method to make content planning efficient is to group it: develop a few "formulas" for the kind of posts you can publish (e.g., behind-the-scenes look, your art in action, user-produced material, close up detail pictures of your work, studio tour, imagery that drives your arts, etc.) and then allocate each sort of content to a different day of the week.

- Use hashtags for visibility

Since the birth of social media, the functionality of hashtags has evolved. While employing a few hashtags is no longer enough to grow a following, they nevertheless serve a purpose: exposing your work to new prospective consumers.

- Collaborate!

Working with other artists can provide some advantages, including exposure to new audiences, affiliation with other renowned artists that can increase your credibility, and the opportunity to meet new people! You can cooperate locally or remotely, based on the nature of your work.

How to Register a Trademark

- Do a Detailed Research

Checking the Trademark Electronic Search System database to see if anyone else has previously registered the trademark you intend to adopt ought to be the first step in registering your trademark.

What is the reason for this? Your application will be rejected if there is a "chance of mix up" between your name and a previously registered or pending trademark. This implies you'll have to wave farewell to your registration fee and file a fresh application with yet another costly application fee.

So, do yourself some good and do as much research as possible on your chosen name. Keep in mind that trademarks that are too identical or generic can result in your application being refused.

- Have the Right Documents

According to Art Law Journal, you should be conscious of a few aspects of the registration before you begin registration.

For example, suppose you consider using your own name as portion of the trademarked name. In that case, you will have to submit evidence of ownership or a verifiable declaration that you declare that you are the owner of the trademark you plan to register, as well as your written consent.

You'll equally be questioned about your filing grounds. If you previously have a trademark for your business, use "actual use," and if you haven't begun selling yet, use "intent-to-use." Pictures of your artwork or even marketing items with your trademark already in use, as well as the date it began being utilized in commerce, will be required when filing for actual use. A good faith statement regarding your plans to use the name is needed for intent-to-use.

You may also be needed to list the goods and services for which you plan to use the name and categorize your name into one of the 45 trademark divisions.

- Register Your Trademark Online

After you've completed your preparations, the last step is to register your trademark. To finish the process, go to www.uspto.gov. The registration process might take a few months and involve numerous procedures, with registration fees ranging from $225 to $400.

The best way to make sure that all of these processes are handled appropriately before, during, and after the registration process is to contact a professional trademark attorney.

Chapter 10:

LEGITIMATE MARKETPLACES

Top Respected Marketplaces

- OpenSea
- Rarible
- SuperRare
- Foundation
- AtomicMarket
- Myth Market
- BakerySwap
- KnownOrigin
- Enjin Marketplace
- Portion
- Async Art

OpenSea

OpenSea boasts of being the world's leading NFT marketplace. Art, censorship-resistant domain names, virtual worlds, trade cards, games, and collectibles are among the non-fungible tokens available on OpenSea. It comprises ERC721 and ERC1155 assets. You may buy, sell, and discover unique digital assets such as Axies, ENS names, CryptoKitties, Decentraland, and more. They have approximately 700 projects, ranging from trading card games to collectible games to digital art projects and naming systems such as ENS (Ethereum Name Service).

Rarible

Rarible is a public-owned NFT marketplace that uses the ERC-20 RARI token as its "ownership" token. Rarible rewards active users who purchase or sell on the NFT marketplace with the RARI token. Every week, it delivers 75,000 RARI.

Art assets are given special attention in the marketplace. Rarible allows creators to "mine" fresh NFTs to sell their works, whether they're books, music albums, digital art, or movies.

SuperRare

SuperRare is primarily a platform for users to buy and sell one-of-a-kind, limited-edition digital artworks. Each piece of art is generated by a network artist and tokenized as a crypto-collectible digital asset that you can possess and exchange.

Each piece of art on SuperRare is a digital collectible, a digital item that is encrypted and monitored on the blockchain network. SuperRare has constructed a social network on top of the platform. Digital collectibles are ideal for a social setting since they have a clear record of ownership.

Foundation

Foundation is a niche platform that brings together digital creators, cryptocurrency natives, and collectors to advance culture. It's dubbed the "new creative economy." It is mainly concerned with digital art.

AtomicMarket

AtomicMarket is an NFT market smart contract with shared liquidity that is used by numerous websites. Anything posted on one marketplace appears on all other marketplaces, which is known as shared liquidity.

It's a market for Atomic Assets, an NFTs standard based on the eosio network. The Atomic Asset standard can be used to tokenize and generate digital items and purchase, trade, and auction items on the Atomic Assets marketplace.

Myth Market

Myth Market is a collection of user-friendly online markets that cater to various digital trading card businesses. GPK.Market (where you can buy digital Garbage Pail Kids cards), GoPepe.Market (for GoPepe trading cards), Heroes.Market (for Blockchain Heroes trading cards), KOGS.Market (for KOGS trading cards), and Shatner. The market is the highlighted marketplaces at the moment (for William Shatner memorabilia.)

SwapBakery

BakerySwap is a Binance Smart Chain (BSC) automated market maker (AMM) and decentralized exchange (DEX). It makes use of a BakerySwap token (BAKE) that is intrinsic to the platform. BakerySwap is a multi-functional cryptocurrency hub that includes a cryptocurrency launchpad and an NFT supermarket, and various decentralized finance (DeFi) services.

Its NFT supermarket sells digital art, meme contests, and NFT in games, all of which may be purchased using BAKE tokens. You may gain bonus BAKE tokens by using NFTs in 'combo meals.' It's also a quick and basic method to create and sell your artwork.

KnownOrigin

KnownOrigin is an online marketplace where you can find and buy unique digital pieces. Every piece of digital art on KnownOrigin is genuine and one-of-a-kind. Creators can utilize the site to show off their work and sell it to collectors that value authenticity. The Ethereum blockchain supports it.

Creators can upload digital pieces to the KnownOrigin collection as a jpg or Gif file, with all files stored on IPFS.

Enjin Marketplace

Enjin Marketplace is a platform for exploring and trading blockchain assets. It is the primary Enjin-based NFT market. To date, it has permitted the spending of $43.8 million worth of Enjin Coin on digital items, totaling 2.1 billion NFTs. There have been 832.7K trades. The Enjin Wallet makes it simple to list and buy gaming products and collectibles.

Portion

Portion is an online platform that uses a Blockchain network to link artists and collectors so they can effortlessly sell, invest in, and own art and collectibles while maintaining full transparency. It features the Artist Community, a global network of decentralized artists and creators.

Anybody could be a collector on Portion. You can keep track of both your actual and digital collections in one spot, making it simple to trade cryptocurrency for art and collectibles.

Async Art

Async Art is a blockchain-based artistic movement. Programmable art can be made, collected, and traded. Both "Masters" and "Layers" are available for purchase. Layers are the separate elements that make up the Master image, whereas a Master is a one-of-a-kind art piece. The artist decides what particular abilities each layer should have. If you change to a Layer, it will be reflected in the Master image, irrespective of who owns it. Artists define the elements of their work and give collectors complete control over any component. They might, for instance, allow users to alter the background, the position of a character, or the color of the sky.

Pros and Cons of each Marketplace

Pros and Cons of OpenSea

Pros

- When comparing OpenSea to other platforms, the platform promises:
- iOS app
- Secure login
- Wide variety of assets
- Configurable auction
- No self-coding minting.
- User-friendly website
- Excellent security
- Low fees & gas free transactions
- Powerful reputation and corporate backing

Cons

The following are some of the cons of trading NFTs on the platform:

- Energy use on the blockchain
- Customer service is limited.

- A cryptocurrency wallet is required.

Pros and Cons of Rarible

Pros

- Non-custodial and open-source marketplace
- Users can design and create their digital tokens.
- A user-friendly experience for non-coders
- NFT or collectibles P2P trading at relatively low costs

Cons

- Bad actors can use the marketplace to gain unauthorized access to RARI tokens.
- Inability to find a whitepaper or roadmap for the project because it's currently in its early stages.
- Rarible supports only Ethereum blockchain network tokens.

Pros and Cons of SuperRare

Pros

- SuperRare simplifies the process of creating, selling, and collecting rare digital art.
- Artists can use the SuperRare smart contract technology to create limited-edition digital artwork monitored on the blockchain, making it rare, verifiable, and collectible.

- SuperRare provides a marketplace for any artist to mint rare digital tokenized art on the blockchain network, which can then be readily traded.
- Most crucially, future transactions continue to pay royalties to the artists.
- It's quite simple to make rare digital tokenized art.
- Strong development team; funds go to the artists, who will profit in the future; authenticity certificates
- Artists now have a new opportunity to market their digital pieces!
- Simple to use (from the artist's perspective).
- Amazing curated content
- Great product development team and a great UX and design team, the technology is more available to artists and consumers alike.

Cons

- More awesome artists are needed to sign up.
- More categories to differentiate artists spatially
- More art will be beneficial in demonstrating the platform's power
- For the time being, only JPEG/PNG or GIFs are supported.

- In the future, some ultra high-definition formats for photography and other purposes could be intriguing additions.

Pros and Cons of Enjin

Pros

- Enjin Marketplace is a platform for viewing and exchanging blockchain assets that is sleek, fast, and responsive
- Exceptionally fast and user-friendly blockchain explorer with no ad
- A contemporary appearance
- Simple, quick, and clean
- The most comprehensive Ethereum blockchain explorer
- Visually appealing and fiercely competitive with Etherscan

Cons

- There is no PC wallet.
- Does not support the ENS domain
- Endless scrolling
- Not as quickly as anticipated
- There are no filters or instructions on how to use advanced search tools.
- No ERC1155...

Chapter 11:
NEW NFT MARKETS

Market Opportunity for NFTs

- Environmental Impact

The blockchain's computer network uses a lot of energy that renders the system very expensive and necessitates that artists pay a particular charge upfront to create their art before incorporating it on the Ethereum network. Some proponents argue that the power consumed is generated at the periphery of power grids and is not the most efficient form of electricity. If there's one thing that each artist I've met talks about, it's that the carbon footprint of NFTs needs to go from carbon negative to carbon neutral. Investors should undoubtedly look at firms, processes, and other methods that can help offset the carbon impact.

- Gaming

Because NFTs are one-of-a-kind, their quantity is limited, and they can only be verified on the blockchain network. What if artists created unique digital items that gamers could acquire and save as NFTs on the Ethereum blockchain? What will benefit from making those works unique if Fortnite sold a skin that anyone could buy for $15?

- Curation and Education Platforms

We've all heard about pioneers like NiftyGateway, SuperRare, and Opensea, but I find hundreds of pages with many NFTs on auction each time I visit those platforms. There is no curation; everything is thrown together, good, bad, and ugly. Rather than assisting a collector in appreciating what they have, the disarray encourages "death by choice." More collectors would be attracted to editorial content that could help individuals comprehend what they are buying, introduce such new artists, and explain who they are and what they do.

- Showcasing Galleries

Where do individuals put their NFT art collections on display? There are a few locations to create, buy, and trade digital NFTs, but there aren't many to display. Mark Cuban has announced that he is launching his gallery, Lazy.com. Cuban wanted a simple way to display his NFTs and include them in his social bios, email signatures, and anywhere else he may put a URL. It is up to the entrepreneurs who can notice the movement to determine how sophisticated these platforms are and how many extra services they can provide.

While the realm of digital art has been since the 1960s, nothing as groundbreaking has occurred in that field until the introduction of NFTs. Understandably, collectors are cautious, while artists are both delighted and suspicious. The realm of NFTs, like everything else, demands dedication, effort, and a learning curve. Early investors have received a huge payoff, and there's usually room for more.

Ways Brands are Using NFTs

The concept of NFTs in businesses can be confusing. The best way to understand anything is to look at examples, which is true for most things. Here are a few creative uses of NFTs by brands. Hopefully, they will provide you with some ideas for incorporation into your business.

- **Taco Bell GIFs**

According to research, 83 percent of millennials prefer to work with companies that share their values. As a result, brands must be open about their support for causes they care about. Taco Bell has been doing this via their foundation for a long time, but they moved it to the next level by selling taco-themed NFT GIFs to support the Live Más Scholarship.

Taco Bell GIFs: How Brands Are Using NFTs

The GIFs were sold out within few minutes of their 25 NFTs (dubbed NFTacoBells) being listed on Rarible. The bidding for each GIF began at $1. They did, however, sell for thousands of dollars each, with one fetching $3,646.

Taco Bell made a wise decision in minting and selling NFTs because it produced a lot of buzz in the mainstream media and social media, which is usually beneficial to business.

NFTs can help you kill two birds with one stone, just like Taco Bell.

- To increase brand recognition
- Support a charity

The two are significant characteristics that can help drum up revenue for your brand.

- **RTFKT Digital Sneakers**

Searching for a strategy to offset the market and build a name for your business? NFTs can enable you to do that. That's what happened when a Chinese virtual shoe firm called RTFKT produced an NFT sneaker for the Chinese New Year and placed it up for sale. The sneaker went for a hefty $28,000.

Ways Brands Are Using NFTs - RTFKT Digital Sneakers

That's extremely good for a business that's only two years old, particularly knowing they sold a sneaker that can't be held, let alone used. Incredible as this was, it was still by far behind the

$3 million they earned with another NFT sneaker they made in partnership with the 18-year-old artist, FEWOCiOUS.

Marketers should jump on board now, while NFTs are still in their infancy. It's an excellent way to get people's attention and grow a fan base. You can learn from RTFKT if you're a marketer looking for new ways to use NFT technology. Create limited edition memorabilia to commemorate significant events and holidays, and use them in your holiday promotion activities. You could give them away to the first X number of customers or sell them separately at an auction.

- **Grimes Video**

In less than 20 minutes, you've made $6 million. That's how much Grimes earned from a Nifty Gateway sale of ten NFTs. Grimes, an artist, recently sold a 10-piece NFT set for $6 million.

People care about NFTs, and businesses can capitalize on that interest to sell their products. You can do things like:

- Collaborations with artists or marketing sites can help you get your brand into the auction.
- Make an NFT and donate it to a charity.
- Organize a contest with NFTs as a prize (to generate leads).

Marketing is all about capitalizing on current movements and using your imagination to capitalize on the buzz surrounding them to draw attention to your business.

- **Kings of Leon's New Album "When You See Yourself"**

The music sector has become extremely competitive due to a large number of artists and bands available. It's not as simple as it used to be to create and maintain a loyal fanbase. The Kings of Leon devised a method of circumventing this restriction. They used an NFT to release their album, "When You See Yourself."

Kings of Leon used different types of tokens for this innovative album release. The first type includes a special album package, while the second includes perks for attending a live show. The third type of token contains unique audiovisual artwork.

While the album is accessible on all major music streaming services, the NFT copy was solely accessible on YellowHeart for $50. The Kings of Leon is the first band to have an NFT album released.

The NFTs were available for purchase for only two weeks, after which no more album tokens were made. The tokens became a collectible item as a result of this idea. The Kings of Leon made history by being the pioneer band to produce a non-traditional edition. More importantly, enabling fans to own a digital collectible cemented their place in their hearts. That is a fantastic way to increase brand loyalty.

- **Beeple Art Pieces**

Mike Winkelmann has become a legend despite being virtually anonymous in mainstream art circles. He was one of the most expensive living artists at the sale time, selling a JPG file for $69.3 million. The file is the first digital-only NFT sold by Christie's and is a work of art sold as an NFT. Beeple sold an NFT painting for more than $69 million.

A ton of offers came in just as the auction was on the verge of closing, forcing the two-week duration auction to be delayed by 90 seconds.

What are the takeaways for businesses?

Be open to innovative ideas and technologies. You should be ready to take risks and be creative in order to surpass the existing competition, which is becoming more fierce by the day.

- **Nyan Cat GIF**

The Nyan Cat GIF debuted ten years ago with a glorious bang on the digital scene. On the cryptocurrency sales site Foundation, creator Chris Torres minted an NFT copy of the GIF, which sold for more than $500,000.

Nyan cat is a GIF that was converted into an NFT and sold for nearly $500,000. Yes, exactly. A vintage animated GIF went for more than half a million dollars.

Chris, on the other hand, wasn't done yet. Classic memes are being sold off as NFTs in an auction he set up. Bad Luck Brian, one of the memes, sold on Foundation for more than $34,000.

What are the implications for businesses?

The takeaway here is that buyers are ready to pay a premium for exceptional service. Transform some of your best ads into NFTs to leverage on this. Make an auction event out of it, and ensure you publicize it appropriately.

Not only will this increase brand publicity, but it will equally allow you to reach out to new tech audiences.

NFTs Market Potential

In recent years, NFTs have experienced massive increases in trade volume and participants. Investments in NFTs increased by 299 percent in 2020, and total sales in the NFT world increased by 2,882 percent in just February. This growing interest is due partly to the growing infrastructure around NFTs, which has enabled full-stack services such as trading platforms, creating projects, and marketplaces.

While some critics have proposed that the recent surge in interest is a bubble, analysts have pointed out that NFT technology is robust enough to withstand a potential crash and is estimated to last for a long time. According to Beeple, a digital artist who recently sold his NFT for nearly $70 million, NFT will be able to back any work or piece of real value. Likewise, Vignesh (Metakovan) and Anand (Twobadour), the current owners of Beeple's world-record-breaking artwork, presume their deal reflects a radical shift in how the world views art. NFTs, they believe, will help to level the playing field between the traditionally dominant West and the global South.

The significance of NFTs as technology would rise as more famous brands adopt the technology. Any type of cryptocurrency, NFT, or standard for capturing a record of ownership is perceived as adoption at the end of the day. DC Comics, for instance, has stated that they are looking into the possibility of selling existing DC artworks based on their intellectual properties as NFTs. NFTs, on the other hand, have applications outside of the art world. Businesses like Tesla or the new breed of subscription-based automotive companies, which are at the leading position in digital transformation, could be the driving force behind such an e-logbook.

Physically accepted derivatives contracts in items, like metals, transferring into warrants at expiry, and demonstrating ownership of the physical asset by the 'long' futures owner are all potential uses of NFTs. These warrants could be presented at the storage facility where the metal is kept. Rights of ownership could be established at this point, and the metal can be practically moved elsewhere. Instead, the warrant may be carried to a bank and used to acquire funds, or it might be exchanged for another warrant in a more suitable place.

While these are simply a few of the countless current launches and discussions, the interest in NFTs makes a compelling case for the long-term transformation to token-supported trading. NFTs technology can redefine how we think about ownership, much like the internet transformed the manner we think about communication and commerce.

As even more sectors, such as music, sports, and others, adopt the trend, technology-savvy people drive acceptance in the art world. Tokens are quickly becoming the most popular way of representing, sending, and trading unique items. There is no question that item digitization is the way of the future, and what we see currently is only the start of NFT trading.

What Happens Next

NFTs allow for the development of previously unimagined business models. Artists can include stipulations in an NFT that make sure they receive a portion of the revenues each time it is auctioned, so they profit if the value of their work rises. Although football teams have used similar contractual conditions in the past when selling on footballers, NFTs eliminates the need to follow an item's performance and enforce such rights on each sale.

New art platforms, such as Niio Art, allow users to prove their own digital artwork easily. Customers who borrow or buy artworks from the platform can exhibit it on a screen with confidence that there are no copyright or authenticity issues since the NFT and blockchain assure that ownership is real.

NFTs allow artists to reward their audience with better media and other benefits. In sports memorabilia, between 50% and 80% of items are regarded to be counterfeit. This counterfeiting issue could be solved by putting these products into NFTs with a traceable transaction record back to the creator.

However, the potential of NFTs extends far beyond these domains since they radically alter the rules of ownership. To develop loyalty in the transaction, trade contracts, and make sure that money changes hands, transactions wherein ownership of an item changes hands have traditionally relied on layers of intermediaries.

In the future, none of that would be required. Since the information on blockchains networks cannot be modified, transactions stored on them are credible. Smart contracts can be used instead of attorneys and escrow accounts to verify that cash and items are transferred correctly and that both parties follow through on their agreements. Assets are converted into tokens by NFTs so that they can be moved around inside the system.

This can change markets such as real estate and automobiles dramatically. NFTs may potentially be a component of the answer for addressing land ownership disputes. Only 30 percent of the world's population has legitimately registered land and property rights. It is significantly more difficult to obtain finance and credit for those who do not have established rights. Also, if we spend more time in virtual worlds in the future, the products we buy there will most likely be bought and sold as NFTs.

There will be a slew of other changes in this decentralized economy that no one can predict. We can predict that it will be a far more open and direct market than we are accustomed to. Those who believe they are witnessing a fad are unlikely to be ready when it occurs.

What's possible for NFTs

There were many controversies when Kings of Leon launched their new album "When You See Yourself" with a collection of digital NFTs, that included digital art pieces. NFTs, which are digital assets stored in a blockchain 'wallet,' is still a relatively new notion for many.

It's no wonder that the NFT industry is thriving now that a prominent rock band has entered the fray. Other musicians and artists have jumped on board. Beeple's "Everydays: The First 5000 Days" sold for $69 million, while a self-portrait by robot Sophia sold for over $700,000.

Some people believe the world has gone insane. Although certain NFTs are trading at inflated prices, this does not indicate that they are poised to burst. NFTs aren't going anywhere. Sure, once the mania fades, certain NFT artworks will surely become less expensive, but others will continue to command high prices in the same manner that 'conventional art' does. As investors develop a better understanding of NFTs, I believe they will grow in popularity as an asset class.

During a media preview of the grand launch of Superchief Gallery NFT, a gallery devoted only to NFT (non-fungible tokens) piece of art in New York on March 25, 2021. A visitor stares at artwork by Hoxxoh. The " Season One Starter Pack" the show debuted at the gallery, which featured a daily rotation of art installations presented on high-resolution 4K displays.

NFTs symbolize a one-of-a-kind item with verifiable ownership rights. You may print digital art pieces, like Beeple's, and put them on your wall — as may others — but you are the only one who can claim ownership. You also don't have to rely on an intermediary, such as a bank, to retain your priceless art piece in its vault and return it when you need it.

It isn't only about digital art. NFTs can be purchased and sold for anything from even tickets to audio clips to an amazing LeBron James slam video. Land ownership and real estate, whether digital or physical, could also be traded as NFTs. A computer-generated image of a house that recently sold for $500,000. The recent offerings and acceptance are still in their infancy, and the possibilities we will have in a few years will be a fraction of what we will have now.

This is a significant achievement for NFTs. They give musicians, artists, and other NFT creators more control over their work and the chance to benefit from it. They are sold directly to buyers, with the revenues going to the artists, a nonprofit, or whoever is named in the contract. For example, in Kings of Leon, all revenues will go to Crew Nation, a charity for unemployed music crews.

Depending on how the NFT is built, the selected donor may be entitled to royalties of up to 10% (on average or more), of any future NFT sale price. This isn't always the case with physical objects like images and music, which are sometimes resold with no money going to the actual owner. Resale pricing for tickets sold as NFTs may be capped to discourage scalpers.

People have questioned how valuable NFTs can be if everyone can create one. Yes, people are turning tweets into NFTs, but it doesn't imply they're all valuable – uniqueness and provenance are what determine value. The only reason Jack Dorsey's tweet is valuable is that he turned it into an NFT. It's unlikely that the NFT would be worth much if anything, if it were made by someone else. Anyone can paint a picture, but mine will never be as valuable as a Monet or a Van Gogh. Something is only worth what someone else is prepared to pay for it at that particular moment. For example, there are millions of baseball cards, yet only a few are 'value.'

Even if the NFT art scene has a bubble, with numerous celebrities helping to expand it, that isn't necessarily a bad thing. The publicity is generating curiosity, which will lead to more education and expertise on the topic. There is likely to be more adoption as people better grasp what an NFT is and the possibilities it might provide, such as royalties for the original creator/designated benefactor. This will increase the chances of finding value in the suitable NFT assets.

Chapter 12:

ENVIRONMENTAL POSITIVE CRYPTO

Going Green with Bitcoin

N orway is the latest country to try its hand at green Bitcoin. Oilfield services millionaire Kjell Inge Rkke, the country's second-richest man, established a new enterprise named Seetee on March 8. In a letter to shareholders, Rk-ke stated that the company's objective is to "develop min-ing system that trans-fer isolated or in-ter-mit-tent elec-tric-i-ty with-out sta-ble de-mand regional-ly. "Bitcoin is a load-balanc-ing eco-nom-ic bat-tery, and bat-ter-ies are vital to the en-er-gy tran-si-tion needed to meet the tar-gets of the Paris Agreement," he writes.

In other words, the goal is to build Bitcoin mining fields in areas where renewable energy farms produce excess electricity during periods of low demand and use that surplus power for mining. The mine receives low-cost, zero-carbon energy, while the wind or solar farm receives a steady, large customer.

According to Alex de Vries, a digital currency economist who co-authored the Joule article, this technique has a great weakness. It is assumed that the mining process can be put on hold when the electricity is required for other, more socially beneficial uses. On the other hand, mining only works if it runs 24 hours a day, seven days a week. Each time miners liberate bitcoin by properly confirming blockchain transactions, the next round of computations becomes a little bit more difficult to break. It's a race against the clock: the only way to beat the competition is to run more machines, more regularly, using the cheapest power supply.

"Each time you closed down, you miss an income level which you never get back" and lag indefinitely, according to de Vries.

The "battery" analogy is also flawed because the same energy might theoretically be used to charge actual batteries, hydrogen fuel cells, or other decarbonization methods should they become more commonly accessible. Still, at least part of the time, certain Bitcoin processes use zero-carbon energy. Some mining enterprises in China switch seasons to benefit from cheap hydropower in the summer and then return to coal. Bitcoin miners in Canada and the Pacific Northwest of the United States are also looking for inexpensive electricity. In a 2019 Cambridge poll of 280 Bitcoin businesses, 39% said their mining operations were fueled by renewable energy.

Bitcoin miners may utilize energy that would otherwise be wasted in some circumstances, particularly with massive hydropower dams in China. Gazprom, Russia's state-owned natural gas corporation, also has a branch that provides Bitcoin miners energy produced from flare gas, a waste product of oil and gas exploration and refining that would ordinarily be released into the atmosphere (although to use it for Bitcoin creates a profit incentive to drill more).

Chia Network

Chia is novel crypto that eliminates some of Bitcoin's issues. Chia, novel crypto, has the potential to solve some of mining's most serious issues while also introducing a new one.

The Chia Network, which was developed by Bram Cohen, the founder of BitTorrent, works on the premise of mining coins utilizing storage space instead of energy-intensive mining equipment driven by graphics cards and ASIC miners. However, there's a snag, and it's bad news for hard drives and SSDs. Given that Bitcoin mining consumes more energy than Argentina does each year, this might open the way for a new, more ecologically friendly age of cryptocurrency mining, one in which significantly less energy is consumed, and gamers do not have to contend with GPU stock shortages and fruitless battles against scalping bots.

Bitcoin and Dogecoin, for example, use raw computational power to execute transactions, which is known as a Proof of Work mechanism. Miners perform these computations, using the processing power of their GPUs and other hardware to collect incentives for confirming and safeguarding the network. The Chia Network, on the other hand, is based on Proof of Space and Time.

Aside from the fancier name, the latter's concept focuses on storage capacity (rather than computing power) to secure the network, rewarding users that grant Chia access to their storage. This "farming" technique varies from mining in that it does not require specialized tools; you may farm Chia using a device from a computer to a smartphone. Nevertheless, the more free space you have, the more probable you are to get rewarded.

Let's start with the issue. Even though Chia is still yet to be exchanged, potential farmers in China are already buying hard drives, and SSDs in large quantities, with prices predicted to rise in response to the increased demand.

Hard disk and SSD prices in Hong Kong, for instance, are expected to rise by 200 HKD to 600 HKD (about $26 to $77). High-end 4-18TB drives are already sold out, and producers are grappling with the same problem that Nvidia and AMD are grappling with in the GPU world: how to limit sales while maintaining sufficient supply to serve the tech-hungry masses.

Environmentally friendly Choice to Cryptocurrency Technology

Stephen Reid, who was elected as the Green Party's nominee for Totnes in the United Kingdom in the recent General Election, is one of the prominent expert of Tools for the Regenerative Renaissance. This program combines climate consciousness with technology and blockchain knowledge.

"Bitcoin was the very first implementation of cryptocurrency and the blockchain technology, and it is extremely energy inefficient," says Reid, who holds master's degrees in physics and complexity sciences. "However, it was a stroke of pure brilliance. It has the same effect on the universe as Einstein's quantum mechanics and special relativity papers from 1905."

"In a style that nobody had thought of before, Satoshi Nakamoto stitched up three or four separate ideas to create the first decentralized type of currency. Bitcoin is extremely inefficient in terms of energy and cannot be sustained in the long run, but thankfully, people have devised even more environmentally friendly consensus strategies."

Proof of stake appears to be the most promising alternative. Blocks are "forged" instead of "mined" in proof of stake blockchains, and instead of addressing difficult questions, the creator of the next block in the chain is selected using a set of randomization and the amount of crypto they own – the stake.

Don't worry. You need not consider the explanation to understand why proof of stake is preferable for the climate. If you're interested in learning more, Coindesk has a fantastic explanation.

Proof of Work Vs. Proof of Stake

Proof-of-work blockchains are planned to run 24 hours a day, seven days a week. Blockchains based on proof of stake only require devices to operate for milliseconds at a time. Proof of stake can drastically decrease the amount of energy required to add blocks to a crypto's blockchain since it does not involve hard computational work. Not using proof of work will decrease the measured footprint to zero and the total footprint by 99 percent.

It's worth noting that proof of stake cryptocurrency's total energy consumption is not zero: it still requires a P2P computer network to validate transactions and protect the framework. Köhler says, "The numbers we determined are 100 percent the mining operation." "The servers that host the blockchain nodes are not included."

Despite this, proof of stake also outperforms proof of work cryptocurrencies like Bitcoin in energy performance. There is already proof of stake cryptos in existence: Avalanche, Cardano, and Harmony, to name a few of the most common – but they are all minorities compared to Bitcoin. Nevertheless,

Ethereum, the world's second most valuable crypto by market capitalization, is in the middle of a difficult transition from proof of work to proof of stake.

The move to proof of stake has three stages, according to Ethereum's site, the first of which is presently live and the third of which is expected in 2022. "Everyone has been waiting a long time for Ethereum to advance to proof of stake, but it will be a long, step-by-step process," says Köhler.

The good news is that if it succeeds, the carbon-saving effects of the change will favor everybody, not just those who possess Ethereum. According to Köhler, "Ethereum is radically different from Bitcoin." "It's a crypto, but it still supports a slew of other applications."

Unlike Bitcoin, which aspires to be the world's largest currency, Ethereum aspires to be the world's largest computer: a blockchain network supporting a programming language. The Ethereum blockchain will theoretically host something that can be conceived and configured.

Countless other cryptos and financial assets, such as venture capital and insurance, are available on the Ethereum blockchain, such as smart contracts, social networking, and, maybe controversially, carbon credits. To top it off, Christie's, a British auction house built in 1766, sold a crypto-artwork hosted on the Ethereum platform for USD 69.3 million on March 11th. Christie's, of course, embraced crypto as payment.

If Ethereum can move to proof of stake, all Ethereum-based applications will be operating for a more climate-friendly blockchain.

Ways Crypto Currency Can Help Prevent Climate Change

Here are some basic areas where blockchain technology can help the environment:

- Managing the Supply Chain

Many people want to purchase ethically produced items, but the knowledge is often inaccessible and hard to verify. Before it enters the store, an item passes through several hands. Companies can easily lie about how their goods are manufactured, what resources and additives they use, where their garbage is disposed of, and how equally they treat their workers.

However, by rendering supply chains more open, cryptocurrencies technology can monitor goods from the producer to the shelf, reducing waste, inefficiency, fraud, and illegitimate activities. They could also help customers gain a greater understanding of how each item was manufactured and delivered, allowing them to make more climate-conscious decisions.

If we monitored food, for instance, buyers would purchase local food items with confidence that it was produced locally. This will also reduce carbon emissions by eliminating the need for food to travel long distances. A fish sold at a fish market could be verified as a sustainable fisherman, or a beverage bag could be verified as coming from a fair trade manufacturer.

- Recycling

People are often unable to engage in recycling schemes due to a lack of incentives. Since the burden for running recycling programs always falls on individual cities, most communities do not have recycling programs. It's also difficult to measure and evaluate the effectiveness of these initiatives. A blockchain-based recycling program may entice people to participate by offering a monetary benefit in the form of a crypto token in return for depositing recyclables such as plastic bottles, cans, etc. Similar arrangements can already be found in some regions across the globe, especially in Northern Europe.

It will make it simple to monitor data such as amount, cost, and benefit in a straightforward manner and assess the effect of each region, organization, or person participating in the program.

Social Plastic (also known as Plastic Bank) is an initiative that converts used plastic items into currency by establishing collection points in developing countries where citizens can deposit used plastic items in return for currency, services such as phone charging, or products such as cooking fuel. They want to reduce poverty while also cleaning up the planet from plastic waste. They're currently developing a blockchain-based app that will enable people to trade plastic for cryptocurrencies.

RecycleToCoin is a cryptocurrency dApp in creation that will allow people to return their used plastic items to automated plants in Europe and across the globe in exchange for cryptocurrency.

- Energy

Conventional power grids are centralized, leading to failures in electricity delivery, such as excess power being left unused. Power failures can also leave people without energy in areas of the world impacted by environmental hazards or poverty.

A blockchain-supported P2P energy system can eliminate the need to transfer electric power over distance, which usually results in losses. It will also limit the need for power storage by allowing surplus electricity to be moved locally from where it is generated to where it is required. Transactive Grid is a partnership between ConsenSys and LO3 Energy that is developing a blockchain technology to address this problem.

SunContract is a P2P energy trading network for solar and other renewables built on blockchain technology. Power plant design is costly, and governments or big private corporations frequently fund it. A blockchain-supported platform will allow institutions, businesses, and people to profit from investing in renewable energy projects in their region and globally.

EcoChain is a blockchain dApp in development that seeks to do just that – provide a forum for individuals to invest in renewable energy and earn a profit. ElectricChain is a crypto platform with some applications, including SolarCoin, that aims to encourage solar adoptions worldwide.

- Environment Treaties

It's hard to monitor the true effects of environmental treaties, and governments and companies don't always have the motivation to keep their commitments. Fraud and data manipulation are equally issues in this field.

Since blockchain allows for the transparent tracking of significant environmental data and the demonstration of what obligations were fulfilled, it could deter businesses and governments from backsliding on their environmental pledges or misstating their achievements. As data is inserted into the public blockchain, it is permanently stored there. For instance, storing legal documents on the blockchain network may reduce fraud and manipulation in the global carbon credits system. The cost of administering this system alone is about $979 million per year. When you have an enormous record of credits purchased and sold, companies and governments are less likely to look the other way when carbon credits are bribed or illegitimately sold.

- Non-profits

It may be hard to monitor where your money goes and how it has been spent whenever you contribute to an environmental initiative. Bureaucracy, bribery, and mismanagement are still prevalent in the charity sector.

Via bureaucratic labyrinths, funds meant to be a reward for environmental conservation or a payment to a particular cause will vanish into unexpected hands, thanks to blockchain technology. In addition to meeting particular environmental goals, blockchain-based money may be allocated directly to the appropriate parties.

Blockchain technology enables money to be exchanged without using a bank account, which is advantageous to citizens in countries where banking infrastructure is lacking. This ensures that money can be sent directly to those in need without going through a complicated network of intermediaries or central authority.

- Carbon Tax

The environmental effect of every commodity is challenging to assess in the current world system, and its carbon footprint is not taken into account in determining the price. This implies that consumers have little motivation to purchase goods with low carbon footprints, and businesses have little incentive to market them.

The application of blockchain technology in monitoring each item's carbon footprint will preserve the data from manipulation. It could be used to calculate the amount of carbon tax to be paid at the point of sale. Suppose an item with a high carbon footprint is more costly to purchase. In that case, consumers will be more inclined to purchase environmentally sustainable goods, and businesses will be more likely to reshape their supply chains to accommodate this demand.

A blockchain-based reputation framework may also assign a ranking to each company and item based on their carbon footprint. This will increase transparency in production and prevent inefficient and environmentally harmful activities.

- Changing Incentives

People and businesses can find it hard to see the direct consequences of their decisions in today's dynamic world. As a result, the motivations for behaving in an environmentally conscious manner aren't always obvious, particularly in the short term.

Individuals and businesses will use a blockchain network to see the true effect of their decisions and be encouraged to take environmentally friendly actions. Blockchain technology can be used to monitor some details, including an item's carbon footprint, a company's GHG or waste emissions, and a firm's overall history of environmental sustainability. Businesses and people can be enticed to behave in an environmentally friendly manner by making details available, issuing tokenized credits for certain acts, or using blockchain-based reputation systems.

Such new incentives can fully transform the drivers of our economy, benefiting us and future generations.

Blockchain, Energy Demand, and Supply & P2P Trading.

By empowering individuals to buy and sell their energy, blockchain technology enables distributed energy production. Traditionally, regional energy systems depended on massive, centralized power plants to generate power and transmit it to residences, industrial, and commercial users through transmission lines. However, emerging clean-energy innovations like wind and solar, energy storage, smart grids, and digital resources like the internet of things, AI, and machine learning enable a larger range of smaller bodies to generate and distribute electricity.

The increasing complexity of energy management necessitates new approaches, one of which is blockchain technology. One way it achieves this is through smart contracts," that enable real-time pricing and render the grid more efficient. They automatically implement the terms defined in a blockchain contract if certain criteria are met, raising productivity and lowering transaction costs.

Additionally, cryptocurrency technology allows individuals to sell surplus power to the grid at wholesale instead of retail rates and local buyers. "Blockchain sheds light on energy demand and supply, allowing for better efficiency," says blockchain strategist Mark van Rijmenam. "By eliminating the need for third parties and lowering cost, it allows P2P trading." Because of this same property, it may be used to link carbon-trading schemes from different regions.

Security risks like hacking and cyber attacks have increased significantly due to sustained digitalization and connectivity. If executed properly, blockchain technology's distributed feature will make networks far more stable. Since a distributed group of peers operates it instead of a central entity or authority, a blockchain network, in conjunction with emerging technologies like AI, can support secure networks and grids, according to the International Renewable Energy Agency (Irena).

Blockchain Technology Application in Energy

"By building the infrastructure to enable individuals to securely and easily communicate with one another without a centralized third party, this technology is creating a new era of decentralized communication and coordination," Irena states in a report on cryptocurrency technology and renewable energy. It adds that crypto ensures protection and data integrity while maintaining privacy.

The technology's potential has prompted an increase in the number of companies seeking to enter the sector. Irena reported that between the beginning of 2017 and September 2018, over 50 start-ups focused on blockchain technology applications in the energy industry, raising more than $320 million.

"Presently, there are over 70 demonstration programs implemented or proposed across the globe, like LO3's Brooklyn Microgrid project, where customers may choose from a variety of renewable energy sources to run their households, and individuals with their solar systems can sell excess electricity to their neighbors," according to the agency.

"With an increasing portfolio of cutting-edge pilots, the Energy Web Foundation (EWF) is developing an open-source, blockchain-supported digital platform for the energy sector. Innogy uses EWF's Energy Web Blockchain, a branch of German power giant RWE, to validate users and handle billing at electric car-charging stations."

Nevertheless, the technology is still in its infancy, and we will have to wait a long time to see if its full potential is realized. "Blockchain has tremendous potential to allow a transition to cleaner and more sustainable decentralized approaches, activate natural capital, and empower communities if utilized in the right manner," according to PwC.

"Nevertheless, if experience has taught us anything, it is that such transformational changes do not occur by themselves. They will necessitate deliberate cooperation among a wide range of stakeholders, from technology companies to environmental policymakers, and will be supported by new platforms." This is what the world of innovation in blockchain technology and energy is poised to achieve in the nearest future.

CONCLUSION

NFTs are a brand-new technology. However, blockchain and crypto have been around for some years. NFTs, like all things related to bitcoin investments, is on the rise. Some are even being offered for sale for millions of dollars. NFTs have been essential in the growth and development of virtual lands, allowing for land ownership in virtual space. Virtual land has a tremendous economic potential since it will enable entrepreneurs to build a solid and secure business for advertising or online sales in the digital space. NFTs create a medium in which tangible objects such as artwork may be taken care of, reducing duplication and confining ownership to the art. This, in turn, generates a scarcity of artwork and, as a result, a value for it.

Tokenizing asset gives investors more control over their assets when they need them. An example is when a virtual landowner decides to rent out his or her virtual space to adverters or influencers for a fee while still maintaining control of the land. In this situation, the actual land still belongs to the owner, but a portion is leased.

NFTs can be purchased on particular online marketplaces. OpenSea, which claims to be the biggest NFT marketplace, and Rarible are two of the most popular platforms. Both platforms allow users to purchase, create, and sell their NFTs. The most straightforward technique to profit from an NFT is to purchase it at one price and then sell it to another buyer at a premium price. Profit isn't a precise science, particularly in a new trend like NFTs.

The ideal technique might be to hunt for digital art that you find particularly attractive or that you think will become more relevant in the future. At best, it's an inexact science, and that is why you should only invest in a few different NFTs. It will also assist in adhering to one of the most basic investing rules, which would be to diversify across multiple tokens.

NFT has the potential to grow and develop the land sector. Pegging NFTs to land parcels has shown enormous promise for growth and development. For example, owning and controlling virtual land gives you the power to decide what you want to do with your land in real estate. You can rent it out or use it to build a robust and secure business for advertising or online sales. This and many others are examples of sectors where NFTs find applications and enormous possibilities.

Printed in Great Britain
by Amazon